'...this thought-provoking book provides valuable insights.'

Anyone who wants to  find this thought-provoking book provides valuable insights. More than self-improvement and analysis, the examples, models and stories provide tools that can be used straight away with immediate positive effect.

Dr Marlene Kanga, Board member
Sydney Water Corporation and Airservices Australia

'...a genuinely useful ready reference.'

Governance functions can be perceived as a 'necessary evil', especially by the operational parts of the business who just want to get on and do stuff. This perception — fair or unfair — can see governance positioned as the corporate cop, or worse, corporate tyrant.

This book provides a practical roadmap, tools and tips for taking your team on the journey from — at worst case — corporate tyrant to accepted authority and hopefully on to the Holy Grail — trusted adviser.

It's not rocket science, and the book's not an esoteric think piece. It's a genuinely useful ready reference.

Lloyd Dobson, Manager Governance

'... it is a win-win outcome for everybody.'

This book is primarily targeted at practitioners, mainly those in an advisory and or management role in their organisations. However, it should also be of interest to academics who want to understand the imperatives driving practitioners, and ways in which they think and work and, perhaps, apply any academic theories to that role. For years, many have argued for greater interrelationship and learning between the two parties. The book is written in a conversational style that is easy to comprehend. I can actually hear Bryan talking to me. In fact, the reason that it took so long for me to read the book is that I was constantly asking myself how had I gone about advising, being advised and persuading over many decades and what I had learnt and should have learnt. The book has to be approached with an open mind. It is a journey that takes time and effort as indeed has the contribution of the author. If you are a 'people person', you will be encouraged and learn - and actually achieve - better results. If you are a more 'results-based person', you will learn, hopefully understand, how you can actually achieve better results. Either way, it is a win-win outcome for everybody.

Pat Barrett AO, Honorary Professor,
Australian National University

'...a simple yet universal blueprint, including examples, for learning how to apply the principles of persuasion.'

After you quit PowerPoint, turn off the projector and end your spiel, most decisions come down to a simple question: are you trusted? This book is a valuable and timely guide about persuasive advising and how to become trusted within the corporate setting. It focuses on the ability to cultivate and leverage trust in order to build and maintain organisational capability and is a great read for those who have to articulate their advice in order to motivate and influence the decision making of others, those in corporate services roles. 'Winning Conversations' provides a simple yet universal blueprint, including examples, for learning how to apply the principles of persuasion. At last someone is articulating the value of trust and presenting it as a core business competency. This is a must read for all in corporate services roles.

Scott Fisher, Group Manager – Zero Harm Risk,
Downer Group

'A simple toolbox and practical guide...'

Winning Conversations: How to turn red tape into blue ribbon is an exceptional resource. A simple toolbox and practical guide that when used individually or with a team provides a systematic and effective approach in developing excellence in influencing and building solid leadership capability.

Christine Campbell, Director, Commercial Operations,
BDZ ANZ

'... presented in a way that humanises the content with memorable anecdotes and real life examples...'

Bryan Whitefield provides an excellent distillation of the latest thinking and insights on the art of effective communication. This book will challenge the way you think about conversations and provide you with the essential tools and knowledge to effectively communicate your message across all levels of business and provide another essential building block to your leadership skills.

What could easily become quite a complicated esoteric subject matter, is presented in a way that humanises the content with memorable anecdotes and real-life examples of winning conversations in action. The practical content and emotive visual examples really resonated with me and will help support the many challenging business conversations to come in my career. While the primary focus of this book is to help individuals whose roles are to communicate and influence important business stakeholders, it will help you with all forms of communication in your life.

This book is a great reminder of how challenging conversations can be, how easily barriers can be put up unexpectedly, and the importance of ensuring everyone is aligned and perceiving your message in a positive and constructive way.

If your role requires you to deliver effective communication then this is required reading.

Mike Shelton, Co-Director,
Energi Design

'Bryan Whitefield uses his own outstanding communication skills…'

This book takes the reader on a journey that provides both the opportunity to reflect on our past experiences and the tools with which to advance and enhance the effectiveness of our communications. Bryan Whitefield uses his own outstanding communication skills to provide the direct pathway to achieving better outcomes from our interactions with others.

Gabrielle Bouffler, Head of Risk and Compliance, DJ Carmichael

'…nail those critical presentations.'

Winning Conversations arms you with the tools to help you nail those critical presentations. It makes a difficult topic seem simple and I like simple'.

Scott Brewster, Director, Umlaut

'I'm now inspired…'

The way Bryan has demonstrated uses of his Pathfinder Model and associated techniques and tools gives valuable insight into skills everybody should learn to harness. I'm now inspired to, and hope to have more, "Winning Conversations".

Philip Reece, Technical Expert, Online Network & Security Operations, Telstra

'I now have a new energy to drive the Winning Conversation ethos…'

In my role I manage and work with a team of 30 people, 50 supplier partners and 6 other internal departments. Managing relationships and conversations is my daily life and the essence of the role and the determination of my success. Whilst I believe I manage this to a high level, I have found whilst reading Bryan's book that each chapter was talking directly to me in my own situation, as Bryan was giving accounts of real scenarios he had faced and how he worked through them to achieve the desired result. Managing people, whether they work for you, with you or around you is the key to success. Bryan's insights have heightened my awareness to continue the path I am on in building strong relationships both internally and externally. I now have a new energy to drive the Winning Conversation ethos and I am inspired to use Bryan's methods for greater success and growth in both my personal achievements and business achievements.

Glen Gregory, National Business Manager,
Technology & Entertainment, Harvey Norman

'This book stands way above many I have read.'

It is probably quite unusual nowadays to have spent a whole working career in one industry. I have, in the corporate travel industry. Now running a travel management company I need to engage in conversations daily with clients, supply chain partners and team-members alike. This book stands way above many I have read. Bryan's 'principles of persuasion' and 'pull strategies' (stop pushing), and the 'persuasion pyramid' are simple and work. I now 'stand in the shoes of others' – and this has made a difference. I have always said businesses do not make decisions, people do. Bryan's approach to winning conversations will help you achieve the outcomes you desire from the people you interact with, specifically your team-members, prospects and clients.

David Lorimer, Managing Director,
HRG Australia

'Winning Conversations goes right to the heart of the problem faced by internal advisers...'

Winning Conversations goes right to the heart of the problem faced by internal advisers within any large organisation, namely how to make sure that our voice is heard. This is no small task, and the unfortunate reality is that the odds are stacked against us from the beginning, with an inherent bias towards assuming that our objectives are not fully aligned with those of the business. It is incumbent on the internal advisor to overcome this bias. By taking a structured and analytical approach to dissect what we need to do in order to earn, and maintain, the coveted "trusted advisor" status, the book hammers home how critical it is for those of us who are paid to be in an advisory role to understand what our internal client wants and needs from us, and to understand the complexity of the various component parts to the relationship. I have provided legal and regulatory advice, both as a lawyer in private practice and in an in-house capacity, for about

20 years, and take pride in providing advice founded on the highest level of professional expertise. But expertise is just one part of an internal advisor's arsenal, and no matter how expert you may be, Winning Conversations shows how, on its own, it is not going to be sufficient if you wish to succeed in developing a meaningful advisory relationship with senior management. The reality is that from their perspective, professional expertise in an internal advisor should be a given. The book explains in clear terms, and with practical examples, a number of tools available to the internal advisor who wants to understand how to take this relationship to the next level, and be part of the team that management turns to in times of crisis or when the bigger decisions need to be made.

Patrick James, In-house counsel and compliance at a global investment bank

Business is moving forward and changing at an ever increasing rate today as each industry in turn is responding to the disruption of digital. What I like about Winning Conversations is that Bryan focusses on the most important skill for everyone in business today – story telling. Being persuasive is essential to getting any business done – whether it is from the perspective of the backroom advisor or the entrepreneur. Bryan has presented a number of well thought through models to ensure the reader can be persuasive and hence fully effective and successful in their career.

Margaret Cassidy, Senior Media Executive

About the author

I am a speaker, author and mentor with a flair for the fields of risk, strategy execution and influencing decision makers. Over my 30-year career I have been a chemical engineer, risk consultant, management consultant and trainer, and there is barely an industry or a sector of government or not-for-profit that I have not had the pleasure of helping. In every case I have found the same inherent challenge: the ever-present friction between the organisation's producing and enabling functions. Those who want to 'get on with the job' and those who want to ensure there is a job to get on with next year and the year after. Almost always, both have the best interests of the organisation at heart, but for one reason or another they do not speak the same language.

From middle-class beginnings (upper-middle, my mother would always say), I have easily floated up, down and across society, learning about challenges, successes and what makes each of us tick. I have learned to speak the language of both front and back office. I have become a corporate translator.

The people I know best and am best able to help are corporate/shared services advisers in organisations of all shapes and sizes. Too many of you are maligned as members of the red tape brigade. To me you are the blue ribbon that makes the package oh so beautiful. This book is for you.

WINNING
CONVERSATIONS

How to turn red tape into blue ribbon

Bryan Whitefield

Published by Bryan Whitefield Consulting
PO Box 7367 Warringah Mall
Brookvale NSW 2100 Australia
www.bryanwhitefield.com
Copyright © 2018 Bryan Whitefield
Bryan Whitefield asserts the moral right to be identified as the author of this work
First Published May 2018

All rights reserved. No part of this publication may be reproduced, stored in a retrieval system or transmitted in any form or by any means, electronic, mechanical, photocopying, recording or otherwise, without the prior written permission of the publisher.

ISBN 978-0-994-52181-1

Cover design by David Williams
Edited by Jem Bates
Typesetting by Letterspaced
Printed by IngramSpark

Table of Contents

About the author	ix
Acknowledgements	xix
Introduction: Leading alongside	xxi

Part I: Persuasive Advising — 1

1: Building trust to get around the hand — 2
- The role of an adviser — 2
- The trust factor — 7
- Finding a path — 11
  - The Pathfinder Model — 11
  - The MCI Decision Model — 15
- Chapter summary — 15

2: The building blocks of persuasion — 17
- The principles of persuasion — 17
- Stop pushing and start pulling — 20
  - Push strategies — 22
  - Pull strategies — 22
- Assess yourself — 23
  - Assessing your influence on key stakeholders — 24
  - Trusted Adviser rating — 25
  - Stakeholder targets — 28
- Chapter summary — 29

Part II: The Pathfinder Model — 31

3: Stand in their shoes — 32

Learning from greatness — 32
- Beauty and the Beast — 33
- Out of the mouths of Belgians — 34

The Persuasion Pyramid — 35
- Personality — 36
- Objectives — 38
- Challenges — 39
- A sample pyramid — 40
- Left brain vs right brain — 42

Show some empathy, for goodness' sake! — 43
The Problem Compellation Model — 46
How people make decisions — 49
- Personality indicators — 51
- Thinking fast and slow — 54
- Emotions rule — 56

The MCI Decision Model — 57
- Motivation — 61
- Clarification — 63
- Level of wisdom — 66
- Implementation — 68

Chapter summary — 71

4: Paint them a picture — 73

Clarity is understanding — 73
- Never assume — 74
- Stirring emotions — 75
- Clearing mental blocks — 75

Painting pictures — 78
- Types of pictures — 79
- Learning to draw — 84
- Why models — 86

What models	88
How models	90
What if models	91
Drawing conclusions	93
Chapter summary	93
5: Tell them a story	**94**
Emotional stuff	94
Connect what?	97
The Story Ladder	97
The Story Impact Wheel	98
Even *you* can tell stories	104
Storytelling guide	104
Construct of a story	105
Ten Step Guide	106
An escape capsule	111
Chapter summary	114
6: Make them believe	**116**
Incredibility	116
Trustworthiness	117
Adaptability	118
Expertise	119
Developing credibility	120
Developing trust	120
Developing adaptability	121
Developing expertise	124
Instant credibility	125
Chapter summary	127

Part III: Winning Conversations — 129

7: Construct of a conversation	**130**
A win-win in 15 minutes	130
Standing in their shoes	131

First impressions	133
Deep listening	133
C-suite speak	134
The rule of three	136
Delivering bad news	137
Painting your picture	139
Telling your story	139
Making them believe	140
'Conversing' with a larger group	141
Plunging in	142
Chapter summary	142
Recommended resources	143
8: The Pathfinder Model in practice	**144**
Practise before you preach	144
The Dreaming	145
If you are a CEO or equivalent	148
Three practical persuasion examples	148
1. Risk management	148
2. Finance — budgeting	151
3. Project portfolio management	153
Recommended resources	155
The wrap	**157**
Endnotes	**159**

List of Figures and Tables

Figure 1.1: Essence of an organisation — 3
Figure 1.2: Essence of internal advising — 5
Figure 1.3: Stakeholder Ladder — 9
Figure 1.4: The Pathfinder Model — 12
Figure 2.1: The push and pull of persuasion — 21
Figure 2.2: Influence questionnaire — 24
Figure 2.3: Stakeholder Ladder — 26
Figure 3.1: The Persuasion Pyramid — 36
Figure 3.2: Mark's Persuasion Pyramid — 41
Figure 3.3: Gray's empathy map — 47
Figure 3.4: Problem Compellation Model — 49
Figure 3.5: The MCI Decision Model — 60
Figure 3.6: Knowledge Circle Model — 63
Figure 4.1: Images of persuasion — 76
Figure 4.2: The push and pull of persuasion (revisited) — 78
Figure 4.3: Influencing from outside the tent — 80
Figure 4.4: MCI Decision Model — 81
Figure 4.5: A framework diagram — 81
Figure 4.6: It's about balance — 82
Figure 4.7: Winning conversations storyboard video — 82

Figure 4.8: VR for training	83
Figure 4.9: The 4MAT Model	86
Figure 4.10: Ladder why model	87
Figure 4.11: The S-curve	88
Figure 4.12: Sample what model for an organisation	89
Figure 4.13: Sample what model for organisational knowledge management	90
Figure 4.14: Sample Venn diagram	90
Figure 4.15: The story of you	91
Figure 4.16: Performance Diagnostic Model	92
Figure 5.1: The Story Impact Wheel	99
Figure 5.2: Storytelling Escape Capsule	113
Figure 6.1: The three main attributes of credibility	117
Figure 7.1: From risk-speak to C-suite speak	135
Figure 7.2: Delivering bad news	138

Table 2.1: Target rating	29
Table 3.1: Extract from Myers-Briggs classification template	52
Table 3.2: Motivation mindset	62
Table 3.3: Level of wisdom	67
Table 3.4: The 7 steps to successful implementation	69
Table 5.1: The Story Ladder	98
Table 5.2: Story collation	106

Acknowledgements

In my first book I thanked everybody. And I mean everybody! And I thank you all again.

However, my greatest thanks go to my family. I have been lucky as a work-from-home parent, as at all times of the day I have been able to watch my immediate family in action. Every one of them is a great persuader in their own right. Without them, this book would not be as good as I believe it is. Thanks Jacquie and thanks Doug, Ben and Emily. Love you all.

A special thanks to Ben, as he is the middle child and you know what that means. He gets overlooked. In fact, both Doug and Emily have a cameo in this book. But not Ben. Bennie, if it's any consolation, I was a middle child too. Kisses.

Thanks Mum. Maybe you overlooked me sometimes, but I always felt loved and cherished and I am sure your ability, and Dad's, to tell a story rubbed off on me. Dad, I am sure you are looking down with pleasure at my work.

To my sister Leslie and brother Brett, I learned a thing or two about a winning conversation arguing with the two of you as we grew up! They were such pleasurable years with all those arguments over nothing, which is as good as it gets.

To all my sisters- and brothers-in-law. You all taught me valuable lessons in life and it is wonderful to call every one of you my friend. And I am learning more than a thing or two from all your kids, a thank you to them!

To my team, Jacquie again and the wonderful Paula, thanks for your support and the hard work you put in to get this book into the world.

And finally thanks to everyone else who helped me with this book. Especially my editor Jem Bates and my reviewers.

Introduction

Leading alongside

Red tape describes what many perceive as the unnecessary administrative overburden that has increasingly pervaded the modern organisation. All caused by the fun police from the back office, those commonly referred to in the modern vernacular as corporate or shared services. There's a perception, in many respects justified, that people from these services often find themselves 'talking to the hand'. The producers in the business are busy producing and ignore you or fight you every inch of the way, even though you know your advice to them will not only help sustain the business but will actually improve its overall success.

In the simplest terms, when you are advising you are influencing a decision. Every one of us has been frustrated when someone has chosen not to take our advice. Whether we are a parent, a salesperson or an internal adviser to a business leader, we criticise them as impudent, misguided or arrogant. Or we defend our failure to get them to listen and act on our advice. How often have you heard these excuses: 'If only I wasn't so conciliatory' or 'If only I had more authority.' Yet if we are honest, we can all name a soft-spoken colleague who can instantly command the room.

Much research has been conducted in recent years into the psychology of decision making. We know a great deal about the reasons people do or don't take advice. And we know each of us has deep-seated psychological biases — some genetic, some learned in our formative years and some a response to particular events in our lives. These biases influence our decision making in positive and negative ways, and represent both barriers and opportunities for those who are seeking to influence us.

We have made great headway in our understanding of influence as well, with the fields of behavioural psychology, marketing and public relations leading the way. Government departments look for ways to influence people to pay their taxes on time; marketing strategists create desire for products we did not even know we wanted; political spin doctors look to swing the outcomes of elections through cleverly nuanced campaign slogans. For better or worse, we have come a long way in our appreciation of how persuasion works.

This book focuses on persuasion 'for the better' and is for internal advisers in organisations. It will help the reflective reader to look broadly at the wider impacts of the decisions made by those you advise, so your advice will be top notch, blue ribbon advice and not be or be perceived to be a recommendation for more red tape. At the same time it offers a simple formula, and provides practical tools and clear examples on how to persuade others.

While the book focuses primarily on persuasion in a business setting, you will also gain valuable insights into your personal decision making and how you can advise those closest to you. But whether in business or in your personal life, you can learn you don't have to 'talk to the hand'.

Another underlying theme in this book is the idea of 'leading alongside'. It sounds simple. You can picture yourself literally standing beside a loved one or a colleague in a meeting room, working through a problem on the whiteboard. We have all been there, and know what it feels like on both sides of the exchange. You know that influencing someone when you don't have authority over them, or you don't wish to use your authority, can be more than a little challenging.

Think about what is involved in the meeting-room situation. The two of you are there for a reason: the person you are meeting with needs to make a decision. Before the meeting starts they may not have been aware of that, or they may have had a different outcome in mind. As their adviser, however, you are there to influence the outcome.

Decision making comes with a lot of baggage. We all have blind spots, and we all have our preferences around how we make decisions. Some of us rely on gut instinct, others on long and careful consideration. Some like to make autonomous decisions, others to canvass a broad range of views and seek consensus. Some demand and rely on lots of data, others scoff at such reliance. Each person's inclination will depend on their background and values, and the environment in which they currently find themselves. Some are hard-coded, some change over time in response to their lived experience.

On the day of the meeting, they are who they are. You have entered the room with some kind of relationship with the person. It could be brand new — perhaps you have exchanged emails, or a phone or video call — or it could be well established. It could be mutually strong or one-sided, respectful or less so, emotionally fraught or pragmatic and impartial.

Let's not forget the important part: the future. In pondering the decision to be made, each of you has to a greater or lesser extent assessed the future possibilities to determine what you believe is the best decision under the circumstances. Each of you, that is, has a vision of the future. In some cases this future will have great urgency — there are serious consequences in play. At other times the future could be more about building alternatives that favour creativity and innovation over a more static environment.

Leading alongside is a simple concept, but the art and science behind it are not. What you will find in the pages that follow will challenge you. You will at times question yourself, your motives and the methods of persuasion you have used throughout your career. By the end of the book, I hope you will have a much clearer sense of how to grow as a persuasive adviser and to deliver blue ribbon, not red tape.

Part I

Persuasive Advising

1

Building trust to get around the hand

The role of an adviser

Everyone is an adviser. Even if you are the CEO or the Chair of the Board, you are an adviser — to each other, and to other members of the executive team and board. As an adviser you seek to influence key decisions. The people we take advice from most readily are those we most trust. To be clear, trust is contextual. I trust my mum, but I don't rely on her advice when it comes to the internet. In the boardroom, a CEO and Chair who trust each other are more likely to get more done more quickly. And as an adviser to the board, trust is your most valuable asset. Hence the original consultant's bible on influencing, David Maister's *The Trusted Advisor*.

In this chapter I explore the challenge of becoming a trusted adviser through the lens of an internal adviser. If you are not an internal adviser, you will soon appreciate that there is much to be learned from the best of these skilled professionals. So don't skip this section — read on while thinking about when and how you give advice in your own role. You may be surprised by how often you do so!

First let me explain the role of an internal adviser in organisations.

Figure 1.1 captures the essence of an organisation. Based on the organisation's purpose, the leadership will set the direction, giving management the flexibility to create strategies that respond to the complexity of the modern world. Some boundaries are established based on an assessment of overall organisational capability. Your advice on where and how these boundaries should be set and your implementation of them determines whether you are creating red tape or top notch blue ribbon service.

Figure 1.1: Essence of an organisation

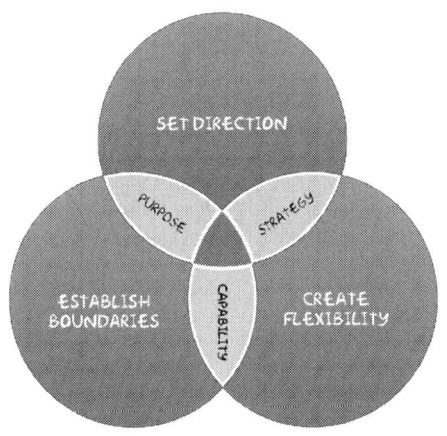

When the leadership team sets the organisation's direction, it can be very specific: 'We are going to be the nation's leading manufacturer of quality beds, with market share in excess of 40 per cent by 2020.' Or it can be much less specific: 'Our goal is to disrupt the bed manufacturing industry in this country through technology.'

When developing strategy, management assesses the organisation's capacity to progress in the direction set while at the same time designing a combination of execution and capability-building strategies.

Organisations usually — or they should if you want blue ribbon — define a range of boundaries. Some are hard boundaries, any breach of which is serious. Some are cushioned: warning signals are provided along the way so management can reconsider their approach according to circumstances. And some are flexible, recognising that speed is important so long as little harm can result.

My favourite analogy here is a naval one. Without getting into technical language, the Admiral of the Fleet may provide instructions to a ship's captain along these lines: 'Captain, I want you off the coast of Okinawa by the end of the month. I know the design capability of your ship, though I don't know the current readiness of the ship or of your crew, and of course I can't predict the weather. So I'll leave it to you how you do it. But do not enter the disputed waters of the South China Sea. We don't want a diplomatic incident on our hands!'

Figure 1.2 depicts the essence of the internal adviser's role, which can be summarised as to advise, guide and monitor. They advise leadership on the direction the organisation should go, based on their specific expertise. For example, an adviser from finance may provide advice based on balance sheet strength, whereas a human resources adviser will have a different view on organisational capability for leadership to consider. And so on.

Drawing on their specific expertise, advisers also propose strategies for management to employ. An adviser from procurement might share information on the strength or otherwise of a supplier market. A compliance adviser might spell out the costs of complying with relevant legislation in pursuing a strategy proposed by the management team.

Figure 1.2: Essence of internal advising

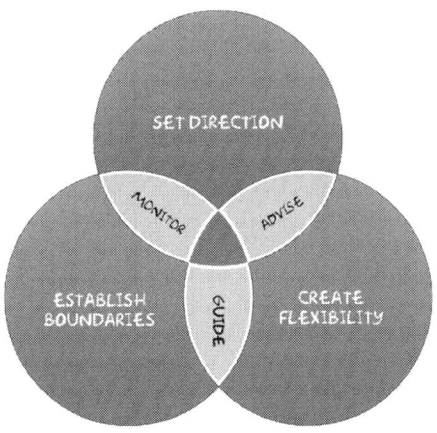

Advisers also offer counsel on the boundaries that need to be established in organisations, from travel and sick leave policies to critical areas such as safety or consumer protection laws, and everything in between.

While advisers guide people in meetings and in one-on-one conversations, they also contribute through the design and implementation of policies, frameworks and processes. In finance, for example, delegation and budgetary frameworks are established, along with processes for reporting on budgets and applying for budget variations. These are all critical enabling systems for organisations and must be blue ribbon and not red tape for your organisation to be as agile as you want it to be.

Advisers monitor the boundaries they have established. Monitoring occurs through a variety of mechanisms, from online, real-time oversight to formal audits.

The critical question for an internal adviser is what happens when a manager, a staff member or a whole business unit breaches one or more of these boundaries? Depending on whether it is a flexible, cushioned or hard boundary, you may be able to work together with the business unit in a cordial and collaborative way to help move things back within acceptable boundaries. It could be as simple as recasting a budget forecast and working out which line items need to be addressed over time to bring the budget back under control.

Sometimes, though, you will need to report a situation to the leadership team. It could be a sudden, unexpected breach that you are obligated to report, or it could be that despite your best efforts, the person or business unit has failed to heed your advice and it is time to escalate the issue. In either case this is a problem for you, because it likely creates conflict and affects the trust the person or business unit has in you.

The trust factor

If your organisation is a well-oiled machine, then providing advice is often the easy bit. What can be harder is designing policies, frameworks and processes that establish boundaries that operations people and staff are generally happy with. Most people resent restrictions that they perceive as obstructing their ability to get on with the job. That's why it is imperative to ensure that when you communicate the need for the boundaries, you show them they are actually blue ribbon and not red tape. Even if you do this well, the most troublesome part is monitoring. Just ask an internal auditor.

I once talked with a head of audit of a top 100 listed company who also had responsibility for risk management. I raised the challenges of the risk management role, when an adviser needs to work closely and collaboratively with a business unit. Because of the audit role, management and staff may be more apprehensive about divulging vulnerabilities. Her reply was, 'I couldn't agree more. I know when I walk through the door they see a big A (for auditor) stamped on my forehead. Their defences are up immediately.' When, soon afterwards, I relayed this story to the head of tax of another large company, he laughed and said, 'You always game the auditor. You can never be sure what they're fishing for.'

It's the fate of the auditor to be seen almost exclusively as a corporate cop rather than as a performance coach. If you are responsible for one of the many support functions that exist in organisations — from finance to HR to procurement and risk — I'm sure you see yourself as a coach rather than a cop, but picture this situation…

You are in charge of business planning and performance reporting, and you are about to meet with Maria, a senior manager, to introduce her to the new business plan format and the process to be followed to create the business plan for her division. Only ten minutes ago Maria had been chewed out by the boss over an issue you escalated last week. What do you think your reception will be? Will she welcome you with open arms? 'Come on in, my trusted adviser!' I think not. There will likely be some hostility there. No matter what you have prepared, how compelling you feel your case is, they will find fault with it, and will likely be vocal about it.

This example points to a couple of central truths about internal advising: it is incredibly hard to be someone's trusted adviser if you are also designer of boundaries that are often seen as red tape by operations people, and it is even harder if you have to play corporate cop!

Consider the stakeholder ladder diagram (Figure 1.3). When the corporate cop element is strong for one reason or another, there is a tendency for advisers to dictate terms when they have the authority to do so. They can soon get a reputation as a bit of a tyrant. Or, as the term *financial controller* implies, they will use their policy and framework tools to control behaviour. When advisers are in dictator mode, staff avoid them. Most advisers, especially those with little natural authority in the organisation, will rely on their expertise. People will come if they need your expertise; the problem is, they may approach you *only* because of company policy. The classic example is the organisation's risk adviser. Their advice is most commonly sought when the business unit has been directed by management to conduct a risk assessment. Usually, this will occur because management aren't confident about what they are being presented with, or because the business unit didn't follow a policy (for example, that all new budget requests over a certain amount need to be accompanied by a risk assessment).

Figure 1.3: Stakeholder Ladder

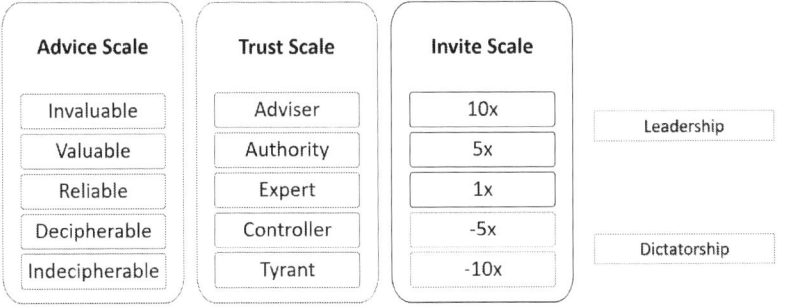

If you provide consistently valuable advice over time, you will become known as an authority and staff will seek you out. As an adviser your main goal is to become trusted, to be seen as someone whose advice has proved invaluable and is sought out time and again. In fact, staff will line up for your advice! But be careful. As one senior leader once told a colleague of mine bluntly, 'Don't call yourself my trusted adviser, please. You become my trusted adviser *at my invitation*, because you have earned it!' Think about the stakeholders with whom you have achieved trusted adviser status, and you'll probably be able to recall how you earned it. Am I right?

So how did you earn it? The answer is through persuasion. Whether you realised it or not, through carefully articulating your case, you persuaded them that they should rely on your good advice. Having arrived at this judgement, they subsequently made decisions based on your advice and had great outcomes. For each stakeholder with whom you have yet to attain trusted adviser status, you must first persuade them to take your advice. If they take it, and it's good, they will learn to trust you.

In the following chapter I will introduce you to the Pathfinder Model, which we will explore in detail throughout this book. This model will help you find the powers of persuasion you are seeking to convince business that what you are offering is blue ribbon and not red tape. I will start with a warning, though. Use what you learn about persuasion in this book with caution. Persuade because it is in the best interests of those you serve. US President John F. Kennedy explains why:

> It is much easier to make the speeches than it is to finally make the judgments, because unfortunately your advisers

1: Building trust to get around the hand

are frequently divided. If you take the wrong course, and on occasion I have, the President bears the burden of the responsibility quite rightly. The advisers may move on to new advice.[1]

Finding a path

The Pathfinder Model

The Pathfinder Model (Figure 1.4) is the key to winning conversations. The model is based on the following three premises:

- Being able to help those you need to influence means getting inside their head so you can find a path through the barriers each one of us puts up to protect ourselves from a poor decision.
- Gaining their trust in your advice is about using tools and techniques to enable them to connect and work with you in a collaborative way.
- Gaining their agreement is about patiently working through options to the point where their choice becomes clear.

The model is simple to remember, so even if you are given only short notice of a prime opportunity to influence a key stakeholder, you can prepare, deliver and walk away satisfied, knowing you not only gave it your best shot, but that you maximised the likelihood they will follow your advice.

If you have the luxury of time, the Pathfinder Model (Figure 1.4), as will be explained more fully in the following chapters, will allow you to build a compelling case in almost any situation. Here I will offer a short summary of the model and what you can expect in the following chapters.

Figure 1.4: The Pathfinder Model

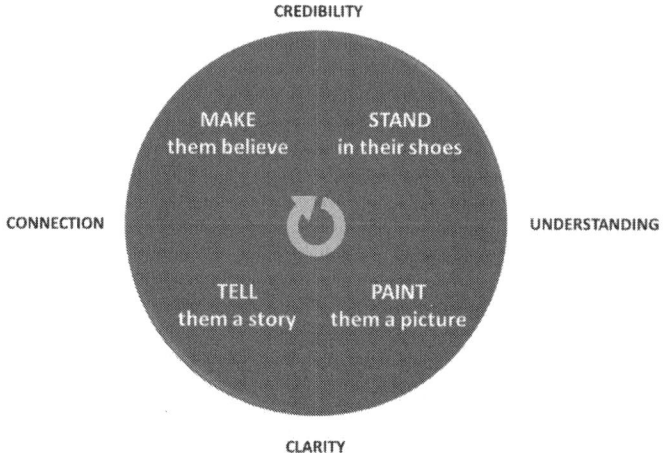

STAND in their shoes

The first step is to stand in the shoes of the person you wish to influence. You cannot align your goals with theirs if you don't fully appreciate their personal and business objectives. Nor can you get past the time-wasting niceties and into genuine collaboration if you don't understand their challenges. And you won't have their full attention if you don't cause them to think differently.

As President Obama said about his change of policy on Cuba, 'When what you're doing doesn't work for 50 years, it's time to try something new.'[2]

Just as important, your ability to influence others will be determined by how well you are able to understand their personality. We all have our likes and dislikes, and our own particular point of view. Knowing what exasperates them is as critical as knowing what sparks their interest. In the chapters that follow I will offer some practical tools and techniques to accelerate your understanding of those you wish to persuade.

PAINT them a picture

We have all heard it: 'a picture is worth a thousand words'. If you ask a room full of people if they are a 'visual' type of person, most will hold up their hand. The reason they do so is not because they are necessarily artistic, but because diagrams and images help them to understand ideas. Intuitively we all know this. I suspect those who claim not to be visual are simply saying they are not 'artistic'. When I have used diagrams or images to explain a concept, those I have spoken with afterwards *always*, without exception, point to or reference those diagrams or images.

I will introduce you to a range of tools and techniques that will help you to present your message in a visual way to those you wish to persuade. I will also do my best to infuse you with the courage to try them out, sooner rather than later. I used to be convinced I could not draw — then I learned I could.

TELL them a story

Decision making is usually a highly emotive process. We make most decisions to make us feel better, whether it is to satisfy a personal desire or, as any CEO would hope, to advance the organisation's purpose. A key component of persuading someone about a decision is to use the art of storytelling to connect with them emotionally.

Everyone loves a good story, but not everyone is a great storyteller, right? Well, that may be true, but you will learn in this book that everyone, even you, can learn to tell a story that has impact.

MAKE them believe

The person you are seeking to persuade must believe in the solution you propose. If you have done everything right in terms of understanding them, used diagrams or other imagery effectively to clarify your argument, and connected with them emotionally through your stories, then the only thing between you and a positive outcome is your credibility.

Credibility has many forms. Reputation is a strong source of credibility. So is the ability to marshal all the relevant facts and figures. What is even more powerful is, having analysed all the pros and cons of a decision, being ready to speak convincingly to each and every one of them.

You will learn about building both instant credibility and credibility over time. More importantly, you will learn that the final element of a winning conversation is to ensure you demonstrate additional credibility at the time a decision is to be made.

The MCI Decision Model

You have probably read quite a lot about communication, influence and negotiation. You may well have participated in programs that aim to teach these critically important skills. So you may look at the Pathfinder Model and say, 'That's what I was taught — and what I do.' Well, let me challenge you on that line of thought.

Persuasion is all about influencing decision making. Do you have a really clear understanding of how people make decisions and of the most common errors made? If not, then my MCI Decision Model will provide you with a critical new piece of the persuasion puzzle.

Decision making is a process. Understanding that process, and where an error has occurred or is likely to occur, is critical to the preparation, flow and conclusion of a winning conversation. Later in the book, when I discuss the first part of the Pathfinder Model, 'Stand in their shoes', I will introduce you to the MCI Decision Model and explain how you can use it to:

- identify the potential error in a person's decision-making process
- create an intervention using the Pathfinder Model.

Chapter summary

This chapter explored the unique challenge of internal advisers in organisations. On the one hand, you want to be trusted by the business leaders you serve; on the other, your role is to put into place policies, frameworks, processes and systems that are often perceived as unnecessary red tape. Worse still, sometimes you need to report that a business leader or their team has overstepped a boundary, which creates the potential for conflict and certainly does not build trust.

I reminded you that sometimes it is easier to get the job done by using whatever level of authority you have to ensure requirements are met, and that this also does not build trust. It drives people away, whereas the trust you build through providing invaluable advice draws people to you.

I introduced my Pathfinder Model. This model, with its four components of Stand, Paint, Tell and Make, will guide your preparation for a winning conversation and ensure what you show and say in that conversation is compelling enough to convince your audience that what you are offering is blue ribbon and not red tape.

My MCI Decision Model, with its three key components of Motivation, Clarification and Implementation, will help you to stand in the shoes of your audience. When getting inside the heads of those you are advising to understand where they may be making an error in their decision making, you can plan your intervention using the Paint, Tell and Make elements of the Pathfinder Model.

Now it is time to remind you about the secrets behind the art and science of persuasion.

2

The building blocks of persuasion

The principles of persuasion

Before we delve into the Pathfinder Model and all it can offer, a quick review of the principles of persuasion will help illuminate why the model works so well.

The most popular book on persuasion is *Influence: The Psychology of Persuasion* by Robert Cialdini. While many PhDs have been, and will no doubt continue to be, completed on how we are influenced, Cialdini's book was seminal in that he collected literally thousands of influence tactics and very helpfully placed them into the following six categories:

- **Reciprocation.** When someone gives us something, we want to return the favour. This is a fundamental human response.
- **Commitment and consistency.** People like to show they are consistent in their actions. For example, if you can persuade

someone to take a small action to protect the environment, they are then more likely to agree to make a greater commitment or at least not to act in a way that would harm the environment.
- **Social proof.** We look to others for confirmation on what we should be doing or liking. Think fashion, music or management trends.
- **Likeability.** If we like someone we are much more likely to listen to them and do as they wish.
- **Authority.** We are more likely to comply when urged by an authority figure.
- **Scarcity.** We don't like missing out, which is why retailers use promotional tags such as 'limited stock'.

To give you an example of some of these principles in action, I can't go past one master of persuasion, my daughter Emily. It was Christmas Day, when Emily was 15, and the present giving was almost over. Torn wrapping paper lay everywhere. My son Doug, who was playing Santa Claus, passed me a weighty parcel with a card that read 'To Dad, Love Emily'. I pulled off the colourful paper and opened the box inside, to find six perfectly crafted 'Reinbeers'. Emily had taken a six-pack of Stella Artois beer and transformed them into a team of reindeer. On each bottle she had glued a fluffy red nose, funny little eyes with irises that rattled when shaken, and red, green and white antlers fashioned from pipe cleaners.

2: The building blocks of persuasion

It was a wonderful present, and I immediately felt the need to return the favour. With her lovingly handcrafted gift, Emily had tackled *reciprocation* and 100 per cent nailed *likeability*. She also scored on *commitment and consistency*, as she had picked one of my favourite vices, beer! It would have been very out of character if I had not been happy to receive beer at Christmas.

What of social proof, authority and scarcity? While perhaps not entirely consistent with Cialdini's principle, I found evidence of *social proof* when I posted a photo of the Reinbeers on social media and had a fantastic response, validating my joy and happiness.

As for *authority*, Emily holds the title as 'most creative and artistic' in the family. Although her brothers Doug and Ben are equally talented in thinking outside the box to create intriguing and fun ideas, Emily stands out through her acting in plays and musicals, her video production and her flair for technology and design. She is *the* authority when it comes to innovative gift giving.

I was now the proud owner of the only six-pack of Reinbeers in the whole wide world (not that I went looking for others). So while I had them they were a scarce item. More so, as they were a one-use only proposition, so as each one was opened the *scarcity* of those remaining increased.

Cialdini dedicates a chapter of his book to each one of his six principles of persuasion, and I highly recommend you read it. While his principles are absolutely on the money and he makes a compelling argument for each, here I would like to offer a different take on them to provide more insight into how you can build influence with people.

Stop pushing and start pulling

I once ran a chemical plant for what was then ICI. I was a shift supervisor on the PA (phthalic anhydride) Plant at Rhodes in Sydney, a zone now redeveloped as a major shopping and residential apartment area. The world changes, and so have I.

When you run a continuous process chemical plant, the money is in keeping it on line 24/7 and running as close to maximum production as you can. In those days, when the pressure was on my style was much more 'push' than 'pull'. 'Move on this quickly, please!' in a loud voice. Of course, contractors did not always take kindly to such pressure, but I had a level of authority that ensured it worked most of the time. After all, they

2: The building blocks of persuasion

were paid a bonus to finish the job on time. But it did not win me their support at other times of the year or in dealing with problems that were not specifically theirs.

Since those days I have learned that when advising others, pulling is more effective than pushing in the long term. Let me explain by using my version of Cialdini's persuasion principles. I have renamed or put a different spin on some of the principles to demonstrate optimal influencing strategies. More importantly, as shown in the Figure 2.1, I have listed them in hierarchical order, moving from push strategies to pull strategies.

Figure 2.1: The push and pull of persuasion

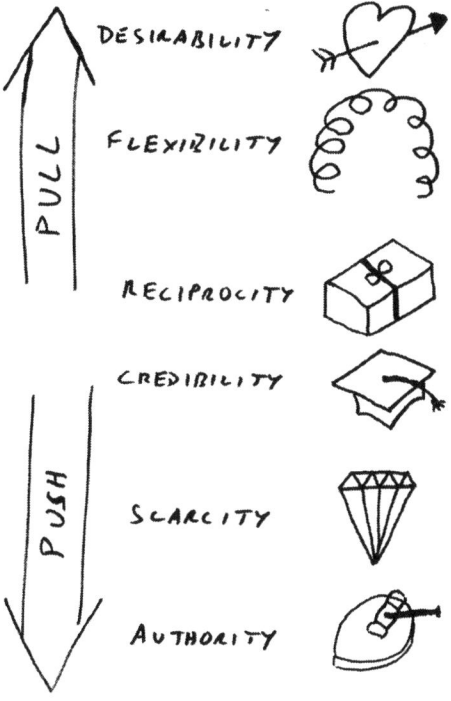

Push strategies

Push strategies are about imposing your will through direction or instruction. At some level, however subtle, force is involved. And if you know your physics, you know every force has an equal and opposite one, where force meets resistance. The following persuasion principles are generally aligned with push strategies:

- **Authority:** Having authority is definitely an advantage when seeking to persuade. Yet everyone is accountable to someone, and authority alone can't be relied on in all situations. Some people resent others imposing their authority and while they will usually comply, they may do so with little goodwill.
- **Scarcity:** Creating scarcity, for example through limiting your availability to provide your advice, may drive people to seize the chance to hear your advice but can leave them with a less than positive attitude towards you, as you have forced their hand.
- **Credibility:** If you have credibility people are more likely to listen to you, but they are not necessarily compelled by what you say. Credibility depends in part on Cialdini's commitment and consistency and social proof. As we will explore later, there are many paths to follow to increase your credibility with those you wish to influence.

Pull strategies

Pull strategies are about motivating, sharing, informing, encouraging people to listen to you and follow your advice.

The following persuasion principles are generally aligned with pull strategies:

- **Reciprocity:** Doing something good or nice for someone inspires them to return the favour.
- **Flexibility:** Be prepared for compromise and don't be greedy. Similar to Cialdini's commitment and consistency. If you first gain agreement on something small and easy, you can more easily build towards bigger goals.
- **Desirability:** I take Cialdini's likeability one step further. If they like you and the picture you are painting of a future they desire, and if you have the credibility to convince them you can take them there, they are very likely to follow your advice.

Assess yourself

We have explored the role of advisers in organisations and covered the concept of persuasive advising as a necessary step along the way to becoming a trusted adviser. I have discussed the risks raised when your role requires you to make the tough decisions and play corporate cop rather than trusted adviser. To help you become a more influential leader and persuasive adviser, I have introduced you to the Pathfinder Model and its key components of Stand, Paint, Tell and Make. I have also reviewed and put my own personal twist on the six principles of persuasion as identified by Robert Cialdini. **Let's now take stock of where you are at as a leader of influence and a persuasive adviser.**

Assessing your influence on key stakeholders

The following questionnaire is designed to identify both how you go about your business of influencing and advising, and the results you have achieved for your key stakeholders. Ideally you should answer the questionnaire for each key stakeholder, as the results will almost certainly vary.

Now grab a piece of paper or your preferred electronic device and list five key stakeholders that come to mind — they may be individuals, groups or entire business units. Next, draw up a table like that in Figure 2.2 below. Using one page for each stakeholder, read the statements and consider how well they apply. Enter your score in the right-hand column — 1 for *strongly disagree* to 5 for *strongly agree*. Then add up your scores for all ten questions. You should have a score between 5 and 50. Repeat the exercise for each of the stakeholders you have listed.

Figure 2.2: Influence questionnaire

		1 = strongly disagree 2 = disagree 3 = undecided 4 = agree 5 = strongly agree
1	I have a strong understanding of the objectives and challenges facing my internal stakeholders.	1 2 3 4 5
2	I understand my stakeholders won't always agree with me. I rarely feel frustrated by this.	1 2 3 4 5
3	I feel excited about many of the stakeholder engagement meetings I have.	1 2 3 4 5

2: The building blocks of persuasion

4	A picture's worth a thousand words, and I often use diagrams and sketches to get my point across.	1	2	3	4	5
5	I love a good story and often use them in my presentations.	1	2	3	4	5
6	I always bring as many of the facts as I can muster to stakeholder meetings.	1	2	3	4	5
7	My relationship with my stakeholders is based on mutual respect, trust and shared solutions.	1	2	3	4	5
8	The change initiatives I introduce meet with low levels of resistance within a few months.	1	2	3	4	5
9	My stakeholders always talk to me before making a major decision involving my services.	1	2	3	4	5
10	My stakeholders often congratulate me on my practical approach to business. They rarely complain of too much red tape.	1	2	3	4	5
		Total =				

The next task is to translate your score into a Trusted Adviser rating. Once you have your rating for each stakeholder you can record it and assign a target rating. Note that targeting Trusted Adviser for every stakeholder is not necessarily feasible or desirable. Read on to find out why.

Trusted Adviser rating

The more valuable and clearly articulated your advice and the more your style is leading alongside rather than dictating, the more likely you will be perceived by your stakeholders as a trusted adviser to them.

Figure 2.3: Stakeholder Ladder

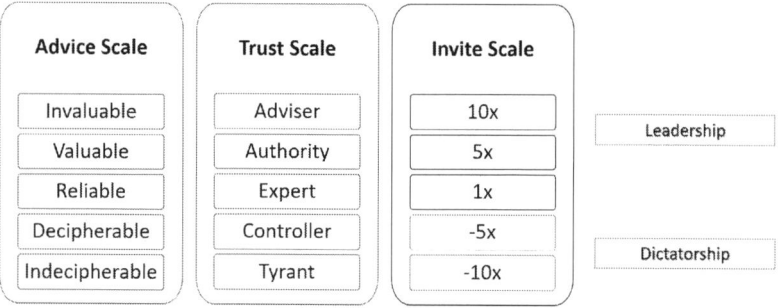

Adviser (45–50)

Congratulations. Your score indicates your stakeholder thinks of you as a trusted adviser. You have built a strong, mutually respectful relationship. You are most likely a highly thoughtful communicator, articulating your message clearly and with passion when the situation calls for it. Your stakeholder has responded to this approach, and you are getting the job done.

Authority (35–44)

Congratulations. Your score indicates your stakeholder has great respect for you as an accepted authority in your field of expertise. To achieve even greater success with your stakeholders, as you read through the rest of this book, think about how you might understand them and their needs better and work with them to find alternate solutions. Think how you can be even more thoughtful in your communication, and ramp up your use of the power of pictures and stories.

2: The building blocks of persuasion

Expert (25–34)

Congratulations. Your score indicates you are most likely working quite well with your stakeholder. Perhaps they present a greater challenge than others and you need to improve how you engage with them. As with the Authority above, as you read through the rest of this book, think about how you might understand them and their needs better and work with them to find even better solutions. And think about how you could be more thoughtful in your communication with them. Increase your use of the power of pictures and stories.

Controller (15–24)

Mmm. Either they are a tough crowd and you have decided on taking short cuts to get the job done, or you have a wonderful opportunity to take a different approach and turn your stakeholder into a believer. Have a really good think about how well you understand them. (Perhaps you don't like what you see.) Exploring the Pathfinder Model as you read through this book, it will help you to put yourself in their position and feel the pressure they might be under. That might change your views a little and give you the energy to try a different approach. Even if they are tough, understanding why this may be so and standing in their shoes creates opportunities to influence them. The Pathfinder Model will help you explore new ways to communicate with them, to reach into their hearts and into their minds.

Tyrant (<14)

Uh-oh! Difficult people, huh? Recalcitrants, all of them! You may be looking at a long road from here, but the journey is still possible. You won't be the first or the last to turn around a tough situation. Time to go back to basics. Following the Pathfinder Model as you read through this book, constantly review how you are working with your stakeholders. Take the time to understand them more deeply and sort out how things got this bad. You need to feel all the pain they feel, especially when they are dealing with you. Only then can you start to make out a path forward. This can be exciting. It's an opportunity to find new solutions to old problems. With some thoughtfulness about how you communicate, the words you choose, the picture you paint and the stories you tell can help you cut through all the history and change their thinking. Give it a crack. You may be pleasantly surprised.

Stakeholder targets

Now draw up a table like the one below and write down your target rating for each stakeholder. There are a few things to consider here. Some stakeholders are more important than others. You may not wish to invest the time in attaining Adviser status with a less important stakeholder, but might rather settle for Authority or even Expert status.

You could find it difficult to develop a personal relationship with some stakeholders. You may, for example, not have the level of seniority that allows you to deal with them directly or even mix in the same circles. Or perhaps your efforts are frustrated by the tyranny of distance or the limited opportunities to engage with them. Alternatively, there may be a potential for real or perceived conflicts of interest.

Put this table somewhere where you will be frequently reminded of it. **All significant achievements start with establishing goals, which is what you have just done.** Now read on.

Table 2.1: Target rating

Stakeholder	Current Trust Rating (1 = worst, 10 = best)	Target Trust Rating (1 = worst, 10 = best)
1.		
2.		
3.		
4.		
5.		
6.		
7.		
8.		
9.		
10		

Chapter summary

Robert Cialdini's six principles of persuasion are a great starting point to understanding how each of us is unconsciously influenced by the actions and words of others. In this chapter

I re-categorised Cialdini's six principles into three push and three pull strategies. The three push strategies reflect some level of coercion that a person being influenced may at some time come to resent, whereas the three pull strategies draw people toward you to seek their advice. The goal is to be as 'desirable' as possible, to provide invaluable advice as you lead alongside your audience.

You now have a benchmark and some objectives. You have identified how close to being a trusted adviser to your key stakeholders you are, and you have set targets for each of them. Next you will learn about the tools and techniques that will enable you to achieve these targets.

Part II

The Pathfinder Model

3

Stand in their shoes

Learning from greatness

The quest for the secret to influence and persuasion has an ancient history. Before we developed language, our ancestors used body language and vocal sounds to communicate with and influence others. Today, for all our sophisticated language skills, our body language and tone of voice remain vitally important in communication and persuasion.

I could have included here a discourse on body language, controlling your tone of voice and conscious selection of persuasive words. There are plenty of books written on these subjects, though. Yes, they can be important, but I believe that being authentic and naturally yourself is a surer path to building trust.

The most powerful emotion you can drive in someone making a decision you wish to influence is trust.

Beauty and the Beast

If you understand the person you are trying to influence and you align your goals to support theirs, and you are sincere in your willingness to serve them, your body language, tone and word selection will take care of themselves. If you don't believe me, perhaps you will believe actor and activist Emma Watson, who played Hermione in the epic *Harry Potter* movie series.

The 2017 MTV Movie and TV Awards were a landmark occasion. The awards themselves had been running since 1992, coming third in status behind the Oscars and the Golden Globes. What made this ceremony special was its celebration of the first major gender-neutral acting award, which saw Emma Watson win as best actor for her role as Belle in *Beauty and the Beast*.[3] And what did she have to say at the awards ceremony?

> 'The first acting award in history that doesn't separate nominees based on their sex says something about how we perceive the human experience.
>
> 'MTV's move to create a genderless award for acting will mean something different to everyone. But to me, it indicates that acting is about the ability to put yourself in someone else's shoes. And that doesn't need to be separated into two different categories.'[4]

There you have it. Great actors excel because they immerse themselves in their role. They stand in the shoes of the character they portray.

Translate this to your work environment. Think about your best outcomes when looking to persuade a manager, team member, customer or supplier. Chances are it is when you were 100 per cent convinced of what was best for them and for you. You did not need to act. Your passion was compelling and infectious. In a one-on-one conversation, a small meeting or a workshop or on-screen collaboration, if you truly put yourself in the shoes of the person or people you wish to influence, you won't need to act or dissemble. Everything will take care of itself. If you are speaking from the stage to an audience of 500 staff, customers or suppliers, however, you may need to learn some skills from acting or public speaking professionals.

Out of the mouths of Belgians

The expression 'Out of the mouths of babes' recognises children's unique ability to cut through layers of adult rationalisation to express something fundamentally wise and true. Here I want to substitute Belgians for babes.

I write a weekly blog. Depending on how much I have struck a chord with readers, I get a few or a stampede of responses. Sometimes it surprises me. One of my regular responders is a Belgian. In one of my blogs I was talking about the need to stand in someone else's shoes so you can understand them before you start to help them. My Belgian reader commented:

> 'In French we have a saying. Before you can stand in someone's shoes you must first take off your own shoes!'

That is so true. Just as the people we are trying to influence put up barriers for protection from poor advice, we too hide behind barriers, protecting our egos by defending our beliefs and opinions. To really stand in someone's shoes we need to take off our own, to stop ourselves from letting our prejudices get in the way.

The Persuasion Pyramid

Standing in someone else's shoes may sound obvious, but I never cease to be amazed by what I find when I try it. The main tool I use is the Persuasion Pyramid (Figure 3.1), which I developed for my Winning Conversations Program. I'll unpack it for you here and explain how you can use it to better understand those you wish to influence.

The Persuasion Pyramid asks you to consider another person's situation at three levels — their inherent personality traits, their objectives and their challenges — each of which has contradictory or complementary elements. This approach should remind you that knowing someone's personality makes it easier to find common ground. Next you need to be certain of their objectives so you can align yours with theirs. The last challenge is to understand their challenges. This gives you credibility and, more importantly, the opportunity to demonstrate how what you want aligns with their objectives. How your red tape is actually blue ribbon. If your advice will help them hit their key objectives and overcome challenges, you will move from *likeable* to *desirable.*

Figure 3.1: The Persuasion Pyramid

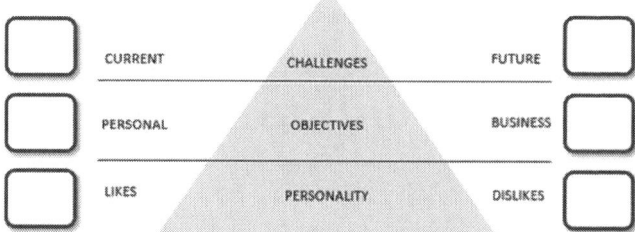

Give yourself a score out of ten for each of the six elements of the pyramid. A score of ten means you understand the person's situation with respect to the individual element extremely well; a score of zero means you haven't a clue. Your result will give you some objectives — to find out more about the person, for example, so you can score 8+ on all of them. An average score of 8+ puts you in a very good position to influence that person.

In the following few pages I outline my thought processes when considering how to score each element of the pyramid and give you some ideas on what to do to improve the scores.

Personality

Wouldn't it be terrible if we were all the same? It would be like having a conversation with yourself all day. You would know what the other person was going to say before they opened their mouth. Fortunately we are a diverse bunch, and that diversity provides both challenges and opportunities for persuasive leaders and advisers. The opportunity is to do the hard, smart work of discovering enough about the personality of those you wish to influence so you can design your approach accordingly.

Right now you might be thinking about personality-type indicators like the Myers-Briggs methodology. We are not going there just yet, as they are rather more complicated than I want to get for now. I am looking at a more basic understanding of the personality of the person you wish to influence (for simplicity's sake, from now on I will refer to them, whether singular or plural, as your 'audience').

The Persuasion Pyramid breaks personality simply into likes and dislikes. Obviously, likes are important. You want to be liked, and you want your advice to be likeable. On the other hand, failure to recognise what people dislike can be the proverbial 'red rag to a bull'. Mention one of these dislikes in a positive way and you can create an impenetrable wall between you.

I usually start by finding out their likes, first in their personal life. Are they a bike rider, a music lover? Do they think and talk about property investment a lot? Then I move on to their likes in the business world. Are they chatty and relaxed at work or are they fixated on time and efficiency?

Dislikes are often harder to discover, as some people simply avoid talking about them. You should be able to pick up some ideas, though. For example, many managers hate people being late for meetings.

I aim to explore their personality as broadly as time and available information will allow. The deeper your understanding, the greater your chances of finding something they will relate to when addressing the *paint*, *tell* and *make* elements of the Pathfinder Model.

What if you have a low score for either likes or dislikes? There are two main approaches to finding out more about them. One is to arrange to have a social chat, say over a coffee, lunch or even a drink after work. This may not be possible given your respective work roles. In that case, your best option is to ask someone who knows them well. Better still, find several people so you can build as clear a picture of them as possible.

Other research avenues include reviewing their LinkedIn profile and reading documents or articles they have authored. Insights into their personality are often revealed in the way they write.

Objectives

People go to work for many reasons. Their business objectives are generally well-articulated. At the same time, they will have personal objectives associated with their work. They may aspire to becoming CEO one day, or they may be trying to improve their work–life balance. Whatever the case, it is imperative that you understand both their business and their personal objectives. If you don't, how can you align what you want with what they want?

Imagine you are in a support function, such as in finance, HR, risk or IT. You have learned best practice in your field and consequently have a firm view of how something should be done. Those you serve may not share this view, however. All they care about is getting their job done. When they need something from you they will ask, and if they don't like your answer they will tell you so and ask if they can do it a different way. They are focused solely on their goals. If you want them to operate in a certain way, you will need to give them a compelling reason.

In chapter 2 I pointed out that while using your authority can be an effective way to get the job done, it is the least effective approach to building trust over the longer term. Rather than telling someone 'they're the rules', it is far better to convince the person of why your way is in their best interests.

Determining someone's personal objectives, like finding out their likes and dislikes, can be challenging. The same strategy applies. Talk to them in a less formal setting where you can ask about their ambitions, or talk to others who know them well. Your research into their likes and dislikes should give you some idea of their personal objectives.

As for business objectives, I like to check if they have a business plan I can view. Better still, can you find out their personal performance KPIs? Again, if you don't know how to source these, you should be looking to find someone who does.

Challenges

Understanding the current and future challenges revealed in the Persuasion Pyramid is critical if you want to be *desirable*. On the top rung of the ladder of pull strategies I introduced in chapter 2, you are not only likeable but, because you are solving their problems, you have also become desirable.

While identifying how to solve current problems is desirable, simply understanding future challenges is important to increase your credibility with those you wish to influence. You will be able to identify challenges they did not even know they had.

How you go about identifying current and future challenges can be very broad. You can research industry news and blogs or conduct your own internet research. I like to search YouTube, as a video is often a valuable way of painting a picture and telling a story. You can also use basic analysis tools such as PEST, Value Chain, Five Forces or a myriad other similar tools. And of course you can go much deeper with your research, for example by interviewing people or holding focus groups, or engaging a research firm to do so on your behalf. Whatever resources you choose to invest in are unlikely to be wasted.

A sample pyramid

Figure 3.2 is a pyramid I completed for Mark, an executive on a leadership team of a large software company. The company was facing significant industry disruption, and if the organisation could not find new ways of operating, maybe even creating a completely new business model, they would be in dire straits. I had only met Mark twice. This is what I learned.

3: Stand in their shoes

Figure 3.2: Mark's Persuasion Pyramid

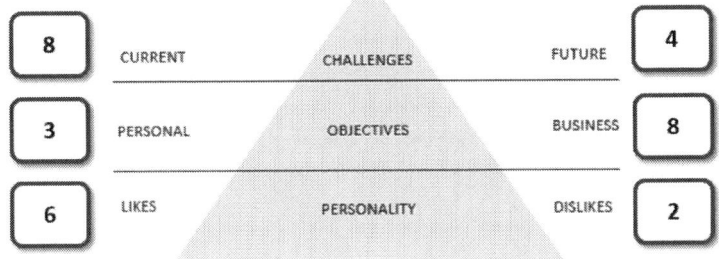

Notes on personality

- In a steady relationship and leading a happy life. A people-person who cares for others.
- Likes travel. Comfortable in his own skin and in his own company.
- Likes reading and talking about business books and what can be learned from them.
- No obvious dislikes.

Notes on objectives

- Personal objectives not discussed. Most likely aligned with business objectives.
- Very clear that the business model needs to change and he needs to find a way to make this happen.
- Currently looking at methods of breaking down silos across the business.

Notes on challenges

- Described the organisation's current challenges in some detail. It is his version, and there may be other challenges he doesn't know about. Need to think of questions to ask at the next meeting to clarify if there are other problems.
- Not familiar with the organisation's specific product offering and market. Research required.

As you can see, my understanding of Mark and his company's situation had room for improvement. I set myself objectives to research current and future challenges so I was in a better position to work on what he perceived as the organisation's biggest challenge. I wanted to be able to demonstrate additional credibility by offering a considered view of their business landscape in the medium term, and to explore Mark's personal objectives the next time we met.

Now try this exercise for yourself. Think of someone you would like to influence more effectively. Grab a piece of paper and start making notes about their personality, objectives and challenges. Then give each box on the pyramid a rating.

Left brain vs right brain

I'm sure you know the theory of left-brain vs right-brain personality types, and that in any individual one side is always more dominant than the other. A left brain–dominant person (say, an engineer) tends to be more analytical and logical in their thinking; a right brain–dominant person (say, an artist) tends towards more creative, intuitive thinking. You may also know that recent studies by neuroscientists from the University of Utah have used brain imaging to study people's brains at work and found no evidence of one half of the brain being more dominant than the other.[5] Despite these results, you and I both know people who more often demonstrate left-brain or right-brain traits, so it continues to be a useful rule of thumb even if the science does not support it.

The Persuasion Pyramid is a left-brain exercise. It is analytical in that it asks you to assess and score your knowledge of a person or group across key domains. But if you are truly going to stand in the shoes of those you wish to persuade, you need some right-brain thinking as well. Enter the Empathy Map.

Show some empathy, for goodness' sake!

A lack of empathy is a serious handicap. Among other things, you can easily hurt people's feelings, and if you hurt their feelings, don't expect them to be too agreeable with you. The first time I learned this was when I was on a leadership development course early on in my career. Our team of up-and-coming managers needed to appoint a leader. Yours truly was selected. We were told we needed an alternate — a VP, if you like. I said to the group, 'Well as I am the leader, I think I should pick my VP, and I think it should be Belinda.' That went down like a ton of bricks. The rest of the team were insulted, not because I picked Belinda, but because I did not consult them. I had just been democratically elected as leader, not appointed as a dictator.

In the debrief with our team's leadership consultant I was able to analyse what had happened and learn a very important lesson. I had assumed that my version of leadership was everyone's, and that I should immediately take control and start making decisions. The team saw me as their representative and expected me to consult them on key decisions. I'm not saying that they weren't aware that sometimes leaders need to make a call, but it was my initial complete lack of consultation that got up their noses. Fortunately we sorted things out and we made a successful team presentation the following day.

What lesson did I learn? The need to consult? Yes, but there was a bigger one. I needed to *empathise* with the team. My assumption about my role resulted from a failure to stand in their shoes, to sense what they might be thinking and feeling. If I had stopped and thought about the situation from the team's perspective, of course I would have consulted before appointing my deputy. We might even have voted on it, which is what we ended up doing. And yes, Belinda was appointed, but I was never quite sure whether that would have been the outcome if I had consulted up front!

Another event in my life further reinforced the dangers of a lack of empathy. This time I was on the receiving end.

On a business trip, I was staying at a hotel on the mid-north coast of NSW. At breakfast, I noticed a group of female golfers sitting near me. They seemed like nice people. When I tried to order another coffee I was told that wasn't possible because the hotel had lost power. On the way out I stopped at reception to ask the best way back to my room, given the lifts were not working. Two of the golfers from breakfast were a few paces behind me. One said to the other, just loud enough for me to hear, 'Use the stairs, you dufus! Must be an accountant.'

What the woman didn't know was that I am an engineer and therefore analytical, and that I have plenty of experience of hotel and office building fire stairs. I know that using the fire stairs is not necessarily a straightforward exercise, and the old building we were in was a rabbit warren. I simply wanted to check the quickest route to my room.

Yes, I admit I felt momentarily angry, and no, I didn't say anything. I simply ignored her. I have long since come to realise that if someone has what seems like an unreasonable problem with you, your best course is to be empathetic towards them, because the problem is theirs, which means they are more likely to have frequent, unpleasant run-ins with people. Challenging them is a waste of energy when there is so much in this world to achieve. **Being able to empathise is critically important when you wish to influence others.**

The Persuasion Pyramid is definitely a good first step in understanding a person. But the better you understand them and the more you can empathise with them, the greater your ability to influence them. The best tool I have discovered for building empathy for a person or group is Dave Gray's aptly named Empathy Map. Gray created his first version of the map when consulting to one of his clients in the 1990s.[6] In more recent years, he worked with the team at Strategyzer, who are creators of the Business Model Canvas, to create the Empathy Map Canvas (download a copy from http://gamestorming.com/empathy-map).[7]

Figure 3.3 gives an example of an empathy map I created for Mark, for whom I completed the Persuasion Pyramid above. Have a look and then move on to my discussion of the process below.

The Empathy Map Canvas asks seven simple questions. As you might expect, the better you know the person you wish to influence, the easier it will be to answer these questions. If you can't answer a question easily, consider it an opportunity to stand more firmly in their shoes. Do your best to find out the answer.

What I particularly like about the way the canvas is designed is that the most important parts are left to the end and that they are graphically portrayed inside the notional head of the person you are assessing. That's right. Most important is what they are thinking and feeling. As I mentioned when I introduced the *Tell* component of the Pathfinder Model, most of our decisions are based on making us *feel* better — hence follow-on question number 7: 'What other thoughts and feelings might motivate their behaviour?' Add to that their 'Pains and Gains' and you have a treasure trove of information from which to develop your influencing approach.

The Problem Compellation Model

Once you have identified the problems of your audience, you need to determine how compelled they are to address each problem. This will guide the approach you take in the *paint*,

3: Stand in their shoes

Figure 3.3: Gray's empathy map

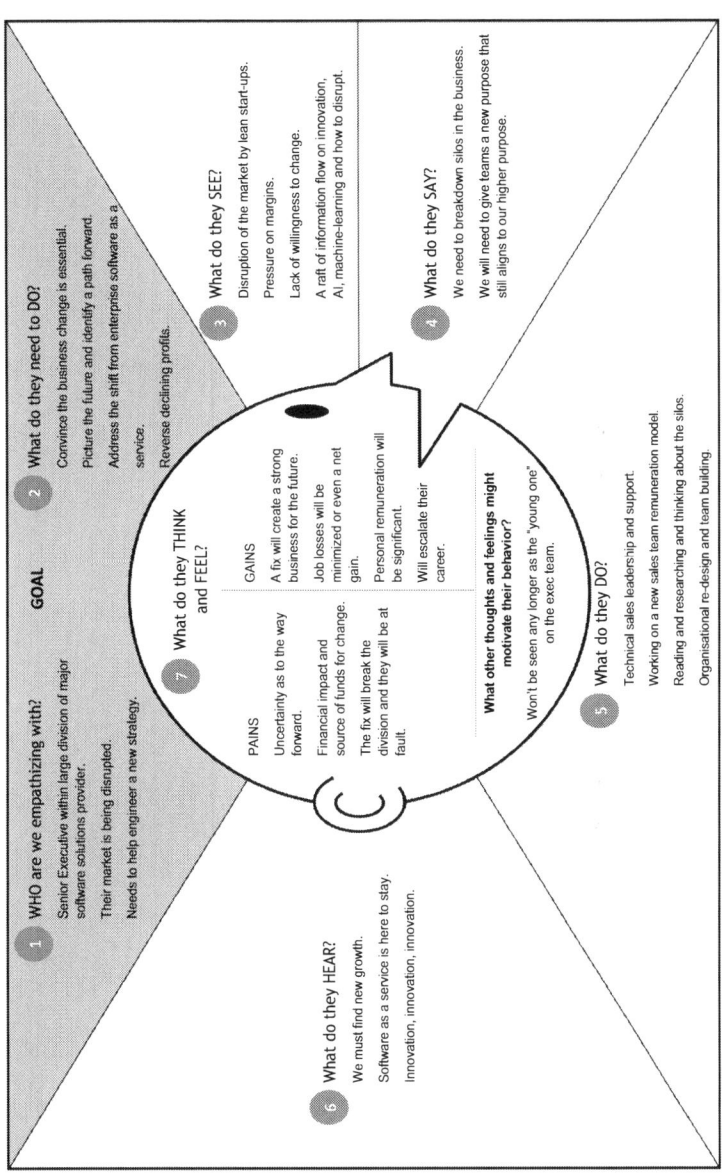

Adapted from Empathy Map Canvas, © 2017 Dave Gray, xplane.com

tell and *make* segments of the Pathfinder Model. I have devised the Problem Compellation tool to help you. It was inspired by a blog by sales specialist Anthony Iannarino called 'Win More by Serving Your Buyers Where They Are'.[8]

Your audience will generally be in one of these three phases:

A. *Problem Compelled.* They recognise the problem and they are compelled to do something about it.
B. *Problem Uncompelled.* They recognise the problem, but they do not feel compelled to do something about it.
C. *Unrecognised Uncompelled.* They do not recognise they have the problem and are not compelled to do anything about it.

When your audience is at:

A. Problem Compelled, you need to HELP them.
B. Problem Uncompelled, you need to INSPIRE them.
C. Unrecognised Uncompelled, you need to TEACH them.

Helping, inspiring and teaching require different approaches. Being persuasive means being multi-skilled.

A. In HELP mode you need to be a *facilitator* and mentor them along the path.
B. In INSPIRE mode you need to be a *leader* and provide a vision to impel them along the path.
C. In TEACH mode you need to be a *trainer* and show them that the path exists and how to find it.

Being persuasive is a craft that you can learn to master. In my experience, not enough of us consider the need to 'sell' our advice when we are influencing or advising. We shun obvious 'sales tactics'. In truth, there is much to be learned from the sales profession.

Figure 3.4: Problem Compellation Model

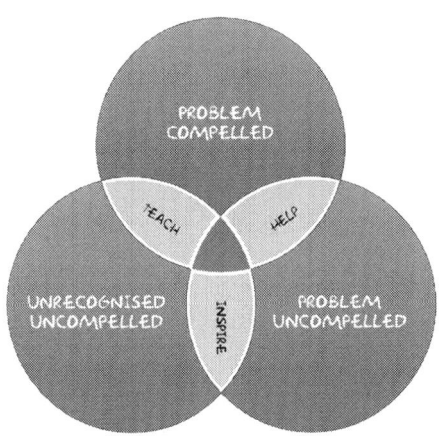

How people make decisions

Now you are acquainted with a few tools you can use to better understand your audience, we can move on to how we might use the information to influence their decisions, which is, after all, what leaders and persuasive advisers are trying to do.

My first book, *DECIDE: How to Manage the Risk in Your Decision Making*, was based on the MCI Decision Model. When the book was published, I took it along to many meetings with senior executives of all kinds and offered it as a gift. If they knew me well, they were usually genuinely interested in the topic. Among those who did not know me well, it raised a key barrier between us, the kind we often use to protect our ego and sense of self. They would give me the look that says, 'Are you telling me I have a problem with decision making? Don't you know who I am, how much I have achieved? Don't you understand I have made it here *because* I am a great decision maker?'

One time I had just finished a workshop with the board of a major charity. The Chair of the Board was a well-respected, very switched on former government minister. I had always seen her as competent and likeable. When I offered her a copy of my book, she respectfully declined with a look that suggested, 'There is nothing in there that is likely to interest me!'

A short time later I was having a meeting with someone to whom I had given the book who, like many others, came to the meeting ready to discuss its concepts. He was the Chief Audit Executive for one of Australia's top ten listed companies. He shared with me that when he finished it he said to himself, 'Every one of our execs should read this book … but they won't.' It was through this conversation that I came to face a widely held article of faith:

> *You and I both know we are great decision makers. It is everyone else who has a problem!*

So I turned challenge into opportunity. Not only was I going to use my MCI Decision Model to help leaders make smarter, faster decisions, but I was going to help people like you *help others by getting inside their heads*. If you can understand how people make decisions, you can better identify any potential errors in their decision-making process so you can help them. As a leader, you need people to decide to follow you. As an adviser you need people to decide to follow your advice.

If you can identify where a person is going wrong in their decision-making process, you know exactly where to intervene. Then you can let the Pathfinder Model do its stuff.

But before I take you through the MCI Decision Model, I need to discuss the large body of work on personality types and how this relates to your challenge of influencing.

Personality indicators

I opened the section on personality with the rhetorical question, 'Wouldn't it be terrible if we were all the same?' I don't draw back from that, and yet the proposition that each of us is a unique decision maker can seem a bit overwhelming if you are trying to influence people's decisions. I mean, there are more than six billion of us, each with our own unique set of preferences and biases.

Of course, others before me have recognised this challenge and have come up with different methodologies to ring-fence people to help us understand some basic tendencies towards certain behaviours. The two most popular methodologies are the

Myers-Briggs Type Indicator (MBTI) and the DiSC Personality Profile. MBTI was created by Katherine Briggs and her daughter Isabel Briggs Myers and based on the work of Swiss psychiatrist Dr Carl Jung. DiSC was created in 1940 by Walter Clark and based on the work of psychologist Dr William Marston.[9]

The MBTI questionnaire classifies respondents into 16 different preferential styles based on the individual's tendency towards either Extraversion (E) or Introversion (I); Sensing (S) or Intuition (N); Thinking (T) or Feeling (F); and Judging (J) or Perceiving (P).[10] For each MBTI classification, identified by a four-letter combination, a description of that personality type is proposed. Here are two examples:

Table 3.1: Extract from Myers-Briggs classification template

ISTP	Tolerant and flexible, quiet observers until a problem appears, then act quickly to find workable solutions. Analyze what makes things work and readily get through large amounts of data to isolate the core of practical problems. Interested in cause and effect, organize facts using logical principles, value efficiency.
ENFP	Warmly enthusiastic and imaginative. See life as full of possibilities. Make connections between events and information very quickly, and confidently proceed based on the patterns they see. Want a lot of affirmation from others, and readily give appreciation and support. Spontaneous and flexible, often rely on their ability to improvise and their verbal fluency.

Sourced from The Myers & Briggs Foundation.[11]

The DiSC Personality Profile, or DISC assessment as it is commonly called, also takes the form of a questionnaire. It classifies respondents into one of four main behavioural types: Dominance, Influence, Steadiness or Conscientiousness.[12] The classic patterns portrayed by each behaviour type are[13]:

3: Stand in their shoes

D: Developer, Results Orientated, Inspirational and Creative
i: Promoter, Persuader, Counsellor, Appraiser
S: Specialist, Achiever, Agent, Investigator
C: Objective Thinker, Perfectionist, Practitioner.

Similarly to MBTI, people are further classified by their second tendency. For example, someone may be classified as Si, which means they are predominantly in the Steadiness quadrant but also demonstrate traits associated with the Influence category.

Having taken one of these tests, you are provided with an explanation of your result that gives you a clearer understanding of how you interact with people and, more importantly, how you may need to modify your behaviour to achieve the best results from working with particular types of people.

The challenge for persuasive advisers is not to get someone to take a Myers-Briggs or a DiSC assessment; it is to be persuasive even when you don't know their personality profile — when you are, in other words, only guessing. Now here is the big secret.

It doesn't matter what a person's personality type is.

While the research shows personality indicators like DiSC are highly repeatable, it also shows that people shift their behaviour based on the circumstances they find themselves in. Therefore in order to influence a person's decision, your main aim should be to ensure you understand their decision-making needs given these circumstances. My MCI Decision Model is particularly useful for this. But let me explain a little more about the shifting in our decision making we all do based on circumstance.

Thinking fast and slow

One man who has spent most of his professional life studying judgement and decision making in the hope of improving the lives of others is Daniel Kahneman, author of internationally acclaimed *Thinking Fast or Slow*. In his introduction, Kahneman summarises his aim in the book as to:

- improve our ability to identify good and bad decision making by others; and
- provide a language that describes what we see to enable conversations that will help us learn the possible interventions that can improve our decision making, or at least limit the downside.

The premise of Kahneman's book is that we necessarily apply a shortcut methodology for making decisions either when we have limited time or when the decision is of lesser importance, and that we use a different approach when we have bigger decisions to make and more time to think about them. He refers to the former as *fast thinking* and the latter, more analytical approach as *slow thinking*. Kahneman suggests the trick to good decision making is to recognise when you are thinking fast when in fact it is a time for you to be thinking slow. When you are looking to influence the decisions of others, it is important to recognise when they are thinking fast when they would do better to think slow.

The act of thinking fast, Kahneman explains, relies on either expert judgement or the use of heuristics. You apply expert judgement when you have such experience of the situation that you know intuitively the right answer or approach. You use a heuristic (in essence, a shortcut or 'rule of thumb') when you don't know the answer because you have not encountered the situation before and you need to use secondary sources to reach your judgement. Here are a couple of examples.

Expert judgement

Firefighters use expert judgement based on processing and absorbing a multitude of chunks of information from which they can detect patterns. It is why they develop what might be called a sixth sense, when the lead firefighter senses it is time to leave the burning building, often moments before the roof or floor collapses.

Heuristics

The availability heuristic refers to our tendency to judge likelihood based on our own experience. For example, how many organisations were slow to take up social media because senior management were wary of it? They didn't understand it and thought it frivolous or childish. Every time an example of social media going wrong for an organisation hit the headlines, they would pounce on it as evidence that steering clear of social media was a wise choice. In contrast, those who pushed past the bad headlines learned to embrace the opportunities we all know exist today. In a more recent example, the scandals of early 2018 surrounding Facebook and their use of customers' personal information was proof positive that social media is bad. While Facebook's reputation took a hit, there are still plenty of businesses that depend on the platform for the access it provides to customers globally.

Now we have covered the fast approach to decision making, it is time to discover the most important impediment to good decision making, even when we have slowed down to think.

Emotions rule

In *Thinking Fast and Slow*, Kahneman attributes the following quote to psychologist Jonathan Haidt:

> 'The emotional tail wags the rational dog.'

Kahneman and his colleague Amos Tersky showed in their early research that some decision making is flawed irrespective of emotion. Later they, along with others, would confirm and demonstrate the true impact of emotion on decision making.

Neuroscientist Antonio Damasio was the first to show that emotions were essential for decision making. In his book *Descartes' Error: Emotion, Reason, and the Human Brain*, Damasio tells the story of a patient whose life had come to ruin. The man, whom he referred to as Elliot, had been successful in business and as a husband and father, until he was diagnosed with a brain tumour. After the tumour was removed he found he had lost key aspects of his ability to feel emotion. He could still dissect a decision, devising multiple viable solutions, but he couldn't actually *make* a decision. By the time he was referred to Damasio he had lost his wife, remarried and divorced again, and faced bankruptcy. No one, before Damasio, had diagnosed a mental health condition.

Kahneman relates how psychologist Paul Slovic took Damasio's findings and conducted a series of experiments to better understand the effect of emotion on decision making in some circumstances. The findings were stark. In the experiment a group of subjects were asked their opinions on a range of technologies and asked to list their benefits and their risks. What they found was that if someone already liked a technology they were overly biased in outlining the benefits and downplayed the risks.

So what does all this mean for the Pathfinder Model? Clearly it suggests that you need to be aware of the emotional state of your audience when it comes to the particular decision you wish to influence. The Persuasion Pyramid and the Empathy Map are obviously great tools to help you identify their likely emotional stance. My MCI Decision Model will provide you with a deeper understanding of the source of their emotional state and any possible error in their decision-making process.

The MCI Decision Model

This model focuses on motivation (M), clarification (C) and implementation (I). *Motivation* creates strong emotions that can either enhance our decision making or block us from seeing reality. *Clarification* is vitally important, because gut feel works only in certain circumstances and is misused by decision makers too often. Also, we often tend to go straight to implementing the first and most obvious solution without considering possible alternatives. *Implementation* is crucial because we are often distracted and fail to stay focused until a decision is fully implemented, and we tend to overestimate our capability in the first place. Let me explain how you can use the MCI Model to identify errors in someone else's decision making.

We all have a natural tendency to think first about implementation of a decision, then seek a little clarification when someone asks for a better understanding of what is planned, while completely ignoring the need to understand our motivation to ensure we are answering the right question and a good decision is made.

So your audience's default decision-making stance is to start by thinking about how to implement the first 'good' idea that comes into their head. They ask themselves, 'How am I going to pull this off?' They may begin with one or two possibilities, but quickly dismiss them. Then comes a seemingly good idea and bang, they are into implementation. Consider this headline-grabbing decision.

The Australian Taxation Office (ATO) identified an issue they wanted to address: that some staff were not recording their work hours accurately. They found some were leaving work early or having long lunches, or having a nice long read of the paper over breakfast after they got to work. What was the ATO's 'great idea'? To send out a memo urging staff to report anyone behaving in this way. Staff are the ones in the know, so this would be the fastest and most efficient way to tackle the problem, right?

Having gone straight to implementation in December 2017, the ATO decision makers woke up one morning in February 2018 to this headline by the (taxpayer-funded) Australian Broadcasting Corporation (ABC): 'ATO urges staff to dob in colleagues who take long lunches, read paper at work'.[14] In Australia 'dob them in' means to report them or, put another way, to 'rat on them'. Dobbing is seen as a very, very un-Australian thing to do. Especially to a workmate, given our working-class heritage that pitted workers against bosses.

If you had been an adviser to the ATO decision makers and you had utilised the thinking behind the MCI Decision Model, your line of commentary, questioning and advice would have gone something like this:

- *Implementation.* Seems quick and easy to implement. But can we take a little time to clarify what the impact might be?
- *Clarification.* I understand the ATO is anti-fraud and all about personal integrity. However, there are some other fundamentals in play here, workplace trust being one of them. If we started to investigate individual staff, what impact do you think this might have on trust within and across teams? How else might we discover the worst offenders without compromising trust in the workplace?
- *Motivation.* Giving this some more thought, let's go back to the source issue. Is it about productivity or integrity

and fraud? If the former, there are plenty of options for improving productivity from staff who may be less motivated than others — from working with team leaders to increase their motivation, to introducing organisation-wide productivity competitions. If it's about integrity and fraud, the first place to start is by looking to influence those who may be offending and don't realise the level of impropriety of their behaviour. And they may not appreciate the impact it has on their work colleagues. This may well apply to the majority of offenders. We can then move to Plan B for those who continue to offend.

With this example in mind, let's explore the core elements of the MCI Model a little further. (If you want to dig even deeper, read my book *DECIDE: How to Manage the Risk in Your Decision Making.*)

Figure 3.5: The MCI Decision Model

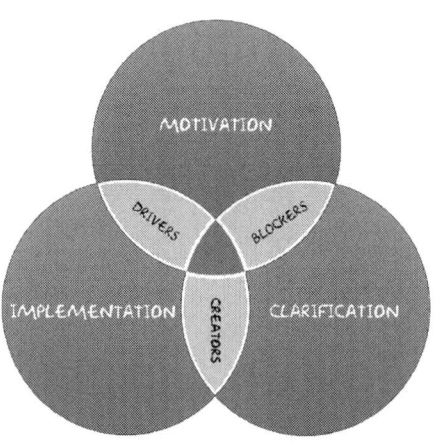

Motivation

As I mentioned earlier, the Persuasion Pyramid and the Empathy Map are important tools for understanding the motivation around a decision. Here I'll give you a framework for categorising the primary driver or drivers of motivation, and what it means for the blockers that may arise to good decision making.

In order to understand the drivers, you need to think of them from three different perspectives. First is from the perspective of *environment*. Think about the environment in which your audience is considering their decision. Is it harsh (a restrictive economic climate, say, or a CEO who is a bully) or plentiful (maybe they are sitting in the research and development department of a company that has just made record profits and wants to reinvest in R&D), obstructive (perhaps the culture is narrow-minded and averse to change) or supportive (it has a terrific internal mentoring program, for example)?

Once you have considered the environment, you need to consider what *incentives* are influencing this decision. Are they seeking physical pleasure or intellectual stimulation, financial reward or some other measure of success, such as more self-determination in their role? For example, their decision may be being influenced by a potential performance bonus, or the possibility of a promotion, or a move into a more exciting area of the company. Perhaps their incentive is more altruistic: they can see how they may be able to make things better, create a happier team, get a clearer understanding of a problem or kick-start a step-change improvement in service for customers.

Finally, how much are their basic *values* driving their motivation around this decision? This might relate to an ethos or set of values they live by (religious beliefs, for example). To what extent will corporate values override personal drivers in this decision, or vice versa?

Once you have explored all of these drivers, you can determine their underlying or dominant motivator, from which you can identify the risks posed by various blockers. Here is a table to help you.

Table 3.2: Motivation mindset

MOTIVATION	MINDSETS	BLOCKERS
Purpose	Think what could be Think what must be	Must find a way — over-eager Single-minded focus — high risk taker
Desire	Nice to have Must have	Need to see value — potentially dubious Very narrow focus — high risk taker
Survival	Win at all costs Fear of failure	High pain threshold — nothing to lose Low in confidence — potential inaction

One final note on motivation. There are three kinds of motivations that need to be aligned for the success of a decision — those of the individual making the decision, of the organisation and of the end customer. If all are aligned, the decision and its implementation can be fulfilled in synch. If the decision maker's motivation is not aligned to the others, it creates a problem in the decision-making process at the outset.

Clarification

There are a myriad ways for a decision maker to clarify a decision. You probably have your favourite analysis tools. Your profession will also provide you with key tools, such as cashflow forecasts for finance and employee engagement surveys for people and culture. As I did for motivation, my aim here is to provide you with a framework to assess your overall comfort level in relation to the quality of the decision process your audience has gone through. You can then guide them if you believe they need to find greater clarity on the pros and cons of the decision.

Figure 3.6: Knowledge Circle Model

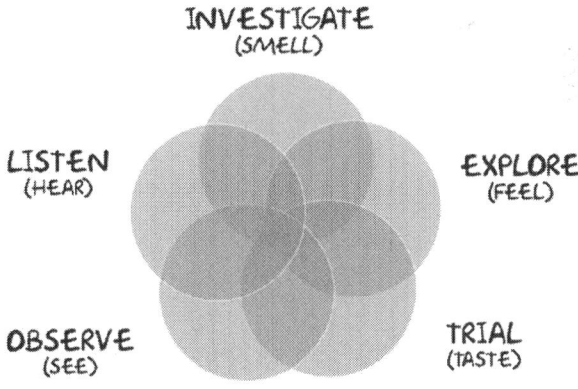

Figure 3.6 depicts my Knowledge Circle Model, which correlates five core methods of gaining knowledge with our five senses. Just as we use all our senses to understand our world, so too should we use all the knowledge senses available to us. We use our eyes to see (which correlates, in a knowledge sense, with our observing things), our ears to hear (to listen), our nose to smell (to investigate), our sense of touch to feel (to explore) and our taste buds to savour different foods (to experiment). Just as our physical senses have been critical to our evolution into the intelligent beings we are today, so our knowledge senses are critical to our evolving understanding of a key decision.

Here is a short guide to using the five senses to enhance your knowledge, especially of those you wish to influence. It will help ensure that as you design solutions you will be designing blue ribbon, not red tape!

Observe

Everything visible can be observed. While some things remain invisible to others, to the astute onlooker there are secrets to be revealed — secrets to success, to failure, to happiness. You must simply open your mind, and the first step is to slow down and look. A good example is culture. The culture of a team, a business unit or an organisation is observable. The way people dress, the factory or office fit-out, the way meetings are held, the marketing material, and of course the way people treat each other. Ask someone to describe the culture of the last place they worked and they will answer you quite readily using very descriptive words. These dominant elements will have survived the test of time, lodged in their memory. Everything visible is observable.

Ask yourself this question. When you observe the culture of your organisation, how is it impacted by blue ribbon? If it is not positively impacting the culture, for example, and people are working around your processes, you may have red tape.

Listen

What is the hardest thing for a leader to do? Are you thinking: fire people, remain calm, manage conflict, make the tough decisions? Or is it something much more fundamental. I believe communication is the single hardest challenge a leader faces. And listening is the first and most critical step in good communication. You cannot properly influence a decision if you have misheard or misread the problem or the choices available. And because every decision has to consider a range of stakeholders' interests, you need to consult widely and listen carefully. As an adviser, you need to point out to the decision maker when they have failed in their listening.

Investigate

When I say investigate, I don't mean develop a research and development budget. I mean don't take someone else's word for it, check it out for yourself. For example, head out onto the shop floor or visit staff at their workstations, and observe them with your processes and systems (your red tape). Don't interfere or correct. Just observe. Does it make sense? How could it be done smarter, faster? Now go further: go talk to a customer or supplier to see how they are impacted. Investigation has no boundaries. You just need to decide how much investigation is worth your while in a given set of circumstances.

Explore

Explore new ideas. What have you not yet considered about the decision you wish to influence? Look for alternative solutions and how can you cut out red tape. While observing, listening and investigating will have provided more insight, sometimes you need some help to open your mind. Use your favourite creative thinking technique. As a minimum, draw a mind map to render all the elements of the decision in one visual representation. You can do exactly the same for your audience.

Experiment

Please, please, please gather the courage to experiment. This could be as simple as walking into someone else's office and asking them if they would agree or disagree with your proposition. Better still, design your own experiment. Experimentation is incredibly valuable. Think about how you might trial your advice to prove its viability and reduce the risk for your target audience.

Level of wisdom

Now it is time to assess the level of wisdom you and your audience have reached. Table 3.3 will help you to score how well prepared

3: Stand in their shoes

you are to provide your advice and how ready they are to make a good decision. It covers data, stakeholders, capability, options and innovation. For me these elements capture the essence of great analysis. Knowledge without analysis is simply information.

Table 3.3: Level of wisdom

Element	Focus	Scale	Rating	Score (1–20)
Data	Data trumps intuition	Absent Interesting Definitive	Interesting — The data is from our existing systems. I lack the external data that would confirm my proposition.	15
Stakeholders	Stand in their shoes	Opaque Hazy Clear	Hazy — Some of the key stakeholders were reluctant to talk to me.	12
Capability	Cascading success	Amateur Competent Expert	Competent — The team has been developing nicely. Some work is needed to ensure all the team members gel.	14
Options	Success by design	Suppressed Explored Designed	Suppressed — I did not make time to work through these and understand what each option truly looks like.	9
Innovation	Turn 90 degrees	Similar Innovative Disruptive	Similar — I did not make time to use creative thinking techniques.	4
TOTAL				54

This table is completed as an example. Recreate it on paper or electronically. For each element in the table, describe the level of wisdom you feel your audience has reached and give it a score out of 20. Then create a new table to score your own current level of wisdom with regard to the advice you are able to provide.

You should be looking for a true wisdom score above 70. Over 80, you are pretty much there; over 90, you are on a winner. The difference between your score and your audience's will indicate where you can help them to clarify their decision.

One final note on clarification. Individuals rationalise, organisations process and customers choose. Don't mistake your wisdom for irrefutable fact. You will need to make sure the organisation's processes lead to full implementation. Finally, your end customer will decide if you're right!

Implementation

The crucial thing people forget when they go straight to implementation is that one big decision is equal in value to the thousands, tens of thousands or hundreds of thousands of decisions that follow. And that value is only realised if those decisions are, by a significant majority, the best decisions for ensuring the first big decision is successful. Table 3.4 outlines a framework to help you assess if the organisation has planned appropriately to execute your audience's decision.

Table 3.4: The 7 steps to successful implementation

1	Document your decision so you can't change the game for convenience.
2	Articulate the purpose so staff can align themselves to it.
3	Craft creative leaders who are willing to experiment.
4	Create challenged teams so they are self-motivated.
5	Focus your people by ensuring actions are aligned with strategy.
6	Measure what matters so you can track success and make adjustments.
7	Close the loop by checking that what you will end up with is what you really want.

We'll now briefly review these seven steps.

- **Step 1 — documented decisions.** Make sure the decision is documented. If you don't, people will be tempted to reconstruct their memory of it at some time in the future, to shift the goalposts to suit themselves.
- **Step 2 — articulated purpose.** Every great program or project has an 'elevator pitch' and a catchphrase. An elevator pitch is a brief (up to 30 seconds), persuasive summation of the project's purpose. The pitch gives clarity to the decision by quickly conveying the gist of it and, more importantly, its value. The right catchphrase can be a 'war cry' for the teams implementing a major decision.
- **Step 3 — creative leaders.** If the implementation of a decision is challenging, your target audience will want to make sure the leaders they choose are creative and prepared to experiment. This is too often ignored. People who like to

experiment are naturally creative. Make sure your leaders have this quality in spades.

- **Step 4 — challenged teams.** Talented teams have the right mix of skills and attitude for the challenge ahead. Based on the clarification you have undertaken, does your target audience have the skill sets needed? Even more importantly, do the staff involved have the right attitude? If the decision to be made does not lead to a set of challenges that allows staff to tap into their intrinsic motivation, implementation will be put at risk.
- **Step 5 — focused people.** A focused person understands and aligns to the project's purpose and strategy and believes in the actions they are undertaking, whether directed or self-directed. Ask your audience if they believe their people will be sufficiently focused once the decision is made. If they have doubts, help them decide what they can do about them.
- **Step 6 — measure what matters.** If targets are not set, progress can't be tracked and teams will be denied an important feeling of reward. You, or your audience, need to measure what matters to ensure successful implementation. Here are three helpful questions to ask your target audience:
  - How will you really know if you are achieving what you set out to achieve?
  - How do you know if what your teams are doing will actually deliver that result?

- How can you know if your teams are capable of doing what they set out to do?
- **Step 7 — close the loop.** Finally, before things go any further, you and your audience need to check one thing. Now that there is a much clearer picture of the outcomes sought and who will be doing what, go back and check if it will fulfil the original motivation behind the decision.

A final note on implementation. At first glance implementation matters the least, because we tend to overestimate our capabilities. Remember, however, that for your customer it matters the most!

Chapter summary

This chapter has highlighted the importance of standing in the shoes of those you wish to influence. It helps you not only to understand them but to empathise with them, to be 'in the moment' with them and to provide advice and design processes and systems that are fit-for-purpose. Blue ribbon, not red tape. There can be no pretence. You should communicate naturally, your body language and voice emanating integrity and trustworthiness. You were introduced to the Persuasion Pyramid and the Empathy Map to help you stand in the shoes of others.

Influencing is all about helping people make better decisions. Understanding personality types aids sound decision making. Heuristics can speed up decision making but can give play to dangerous psychological biases. Most often emotions, rather than logic, rule decisions.

Using the MCI Decision Model will help you understand where your audience may be making an error in their decision-making process. Exploring motivation, clarification and implementation will help you identify potential errors in the decision making of others and build the quality of your advice.

With this new understanding of your audience and what you need to influence them about, and this range of tools to work with, it is time to move on to the *how* of influencing.

Recommended resources

Oscar Trimboli. 'Deep Listening Podcast'. www.oscartrimboli.com

Anthony Iannarino (2016). *The Only Sales Guide You'll Ever Need*, Portfolio.

Bryan Whitefield (2015). *DECIDE: How to Manage the Risk in Your Decision Making*.

4

Paint them a picture

Clarity is understanding

The old saying that a picture's worth a thousand words is so true. Pictures can capture complex meaning in a snapshot. Let's say I told you I drove to work today. If you were meeting me for the first time you would probably picture a vehicle in your mind based on how I look — that is, your initial perceptions of me. If I was wearing a suit you might imagine me in a nice sedan. If it was an Armani suit, you might picture me in a high-end vehicle, maybe a Ferrari if I looked swish enough or a Rolls-Royce if I was particularly affluent and distinguished looking. If I wore a high-visibility vest and work boots you might imagine a utility vehicle.

How often have you been wrong about someone based on appearance? More than once, I expect. We all have.

We have already covered the value of standing in the shoes of those you wish to influence in order to understand them.

You also need to paint them a picture to make sure they understand YOU.

Never assume

I have used the same travel agent for over twenty years. As it happens, his name is Bryan too. My wife, then girlfriend, went into his travel agency in the early nineties to organise a trip to visit her family back in Canada. A year or two later he helped us organise our honeymoon. Bryan has given us impeccable service ever since, and I still book all my business travel through him.

I speak with Bryan on the phone regularly, yet I have never met him. There has never been the need, as all transactions can be done over the phone and by email. I feel I know him well, though. He has kids about the same age as mine. He has visited many of the places we travel to, and he has always given good advice on what to do and what to expect. This was more important when our kids were young and travelling was more challenging, since he was in the same boat, and so he became our trusted travel adviser.

One day earlier this year a strange thing happened. I saw Bryan for the very first time — not in person, but he had included a photo of himself in his email signature. I was floored. Over the twenty years I had been speaking with him I had developed a mental image, and it turned out he was nothing like I had imagined. Not that he looks like an ogre, or George Clooney. Just a regular guy about my age. I just wasn't expecting him to look like he does. I had done what everyone does in the absence of a picture: I formed one in my mind — my version of reality, which was disrupted entirely by a photo of the real Bryan.

So if you're thinking I don't need to draw you a picture because I explain things really well, think again. Never assume. People will form their own mental picture if you don't give them a more accurate one.

Stirring emotions

In telling this story, I used the words 'a strange thing happened'. Why? Because of how seeing Bryan for the first time in that photo made me *feel*. The picture created a weird emotion in me, completely disrupting the mental picture I had. And we already know that emotions rule.

> *Pictures trigger emotional responses, and our emotions heavily influence our decisions.*

Clearing mental blocks

Remember my version of the six principles of persuasion? Can you list them? Have a go on a piece of paper or your electronic device now.

Having a little trouble? Now look at the six images in Figure 4.1. I use these images to remind me of the six principles. Why? Because when I started listing them in my training programs I would often get a mental block. Crazy, I know, but that was how it was. By associating an image with each principle I was able to recall each one easily, every time.

Figure 4.1: Images of persuasion

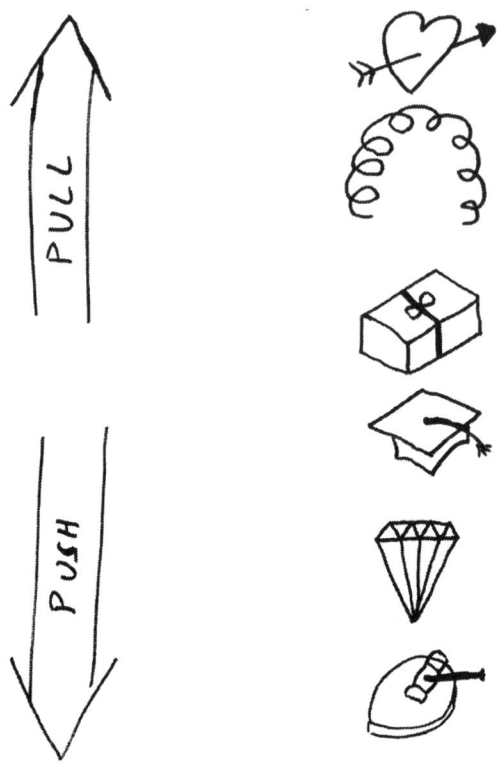

Let's see if it helps you. Look at each of the images of persuasion in Figure 4.1. What does it remind you of about the science of persuasion? Go back to your list and add to or revise it. Now turn to Figure 4.2 to reacquaint yourself with the push and pull of persuasion diagram from chapter 2, and see how well you have remembered them.

If you are like most people who have not already studied Cialdini's six principles, you will have struggled to list all six.

4: Paint them a picture

The images make it easier for you either to nail the list or to think of a word or a term closer to mine or Cialdini's.

Pictures, especially if hand drawn, help us remember things. The act of drawing has an impact on the brain. Research has shown that the retention rate for information presented without pictures or diagrams is 10 per cent after three days, while for the same information with pictures or diagrams, the retention rate increases to a whopping 65 per cent — six and a half times that of the information-only approach.[15]

This is important for two reasons. Firstly, the person you are wishing to persuade can recall and therefore apply your advice more easily. Secondly, often a person you need to persuade to take a course of action will have to persuade others. A team leader, for example, may need to persuade their team to change course because of your advice. With visual reference points, they are more easily able to brief their team by using these visuals, or they will simply have a stronger memory of your key points.

Now I have painted a picture of why you need to use pictures, let me help you build your picture-painting repertoire. And by the way, research also shows that when it comes to drawing diagrams, the quality of the diagram has no effect on a person's ability to remember it.[16] So don't skip the next section with a 'but I can't draw' thing going on in your head. You can, and I'll show you how.

Figure 4.2: The push and pull of persuasion (revisited)

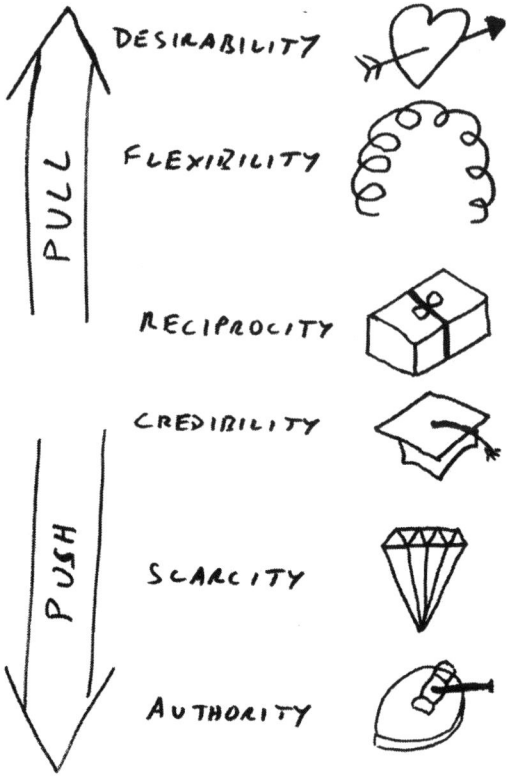

Painting pictures

The person who brought to my attention the power of images to persuade is Matt Church. While Matt is known to many as a motivational speaker, he is also founded Thought Leaders back in 2000.

I've been a student of Matt's at Thought Leaders Business School, a place where solopreneurs come together to learn and share ideas to help our consulting practices prosper. And I've recently had the honour of being invited onto the Thought Leaders Business School faculty.

Absolutely the most powerful skill I developed from working with Matt was using visual communication to help persuade others. Much of what I am about to explain about painting pictures I learned from Matt and many other people at Thought Leaders.

Types of pictures

Painting a picture is easier than you might think. If you are prepared to make the commitment, there are specialist firms who can help you with virtual reality and video production, or you can purchase video storyboarding software. I am not going to go into these options here, as my focus is on one-on-one or one-on-a-few conversations. Generally, that means you are going to either sketch or draw diagrams and models, or show pictures. You may do this on paper, using your drawing app on your device, or on a whiteboard or smartboard.

Let's deal quickly with pictures first before we get into the heavy lifting that will require more thought and practice.

There is one simple rule when using a picture: ask *why* you want to use it. If it is because you think you can't adequately draw what the picture portrays, then you are taking the easy way out, which will potentially reduce your level of influence. Drawing is much more effective.

There are only two reasons why you should show a picture. The first is that your 'conversation' is with a large group, you need to use audio-visual equipment and you don't have the technology to draw on the screen. If possible, get this equipment. The second and much better reason is that you want to show them something real. Think about how charities try to influence us to donate. Seeing pictures of a sick or disadvantaged child pulls at our heart strings. If you have a photo that shows the reality of a situation you are describing, use it. If you don't, then go back to drawing sketches, models and diagrams.

There are many types of images you can present, including drawings, models, diagrams, photos, videos and virtual reality. Each can play an important role in helping others understand your vision of the future and motivating them so they remember you and your advice.

Below are some examples:

- **Sketch.** A drawing may depict objects and/or people. Sketches are very good for conveying concepts. You can sketch up a whole story if you wish to.

Figure 4.3: Influencing from outside the tent

4: Paint them a picture

- **Model.** Best used to communicate quickly and succinctly, a model is a simplified representation of a concept, process or system.

Figure 4.4: MCI Decision Model

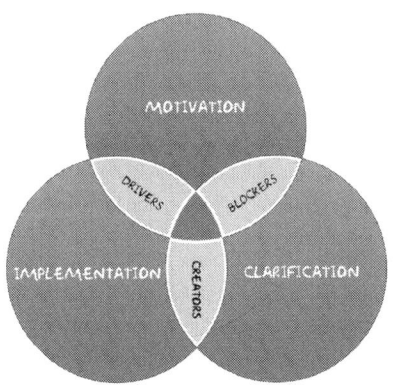

- **Diagram.** Most often clearly instructional, a diagram is a drawing using shapes and text labels. A framework diagram, for example, is often preceded by simpler models to convey the underlying principles on which the framework is based.

Figure 4.5: A framework diagram

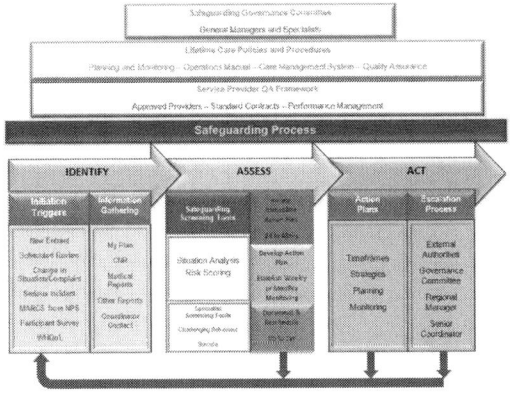

- **Pictures.** Photographs, the most commonly used picture type, can be used in much the same way as a sketch or a model, but convey a more vibrant, lifelike image. The downside is that it is less interactive, which means you cannot unveil your argument or concept gradually, step by step.

Figure 4.6: It's about balance

- **Video.** The great power of the video is its ability to portray people, activities and ideas graphically and realistically. It can also include still photos, drawings and text. Again, you can sketch up a full storyboard.

Figure 4.7: Winning conversations storyboard video

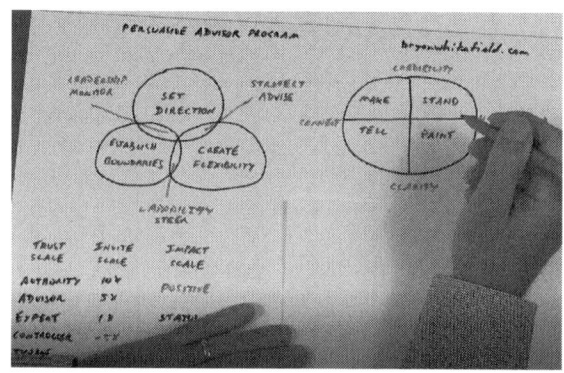

4: Paint them a picture

- **Virtual Reality (VR).** This medium will increasingly become the go-to means of visualising your communication. Already real estate agents use immersive 3D technology to offer prospective buyers a virtual tour of the home. The house is filmed with a 3D camera, and by wearing a VR headset you can 'walk through' the house. VR is also being used in training programs, in particular for high-risk occupations such as mining, where workers are taught to recognise and respond appropriately to the hazardous conditions they might encounter in the workplace. It won't be long before we can work up a VR presentation as easily as we work up a PowerPoint presentation.

Figure 4.8: VR for training

Learning to draw

If drawing doesn't come naturally to you, you are probably in need of a few tips. Here are mine for sketching and for drawing models and diagrams.

Sketching

When sketching, the first rule is to keep it simple. To draw people, use stick figures. The second rule is if you need to draw something a little more complicated, make sure you *practise* until you can draw it quickly and easily. The third rule is my favourite. You can learn how to draw any object you like simply by searching the internet. When I wanted a symbol to depict my fourth principle of persuasion, credibility, I thought to myself how well eminent academics represent credibility. What about drawing a mortarboard? I Googled 'how to draw an academic's hat' and was pointed to 'How to draw a graduation cap' in wikiHow.[17] Simple!

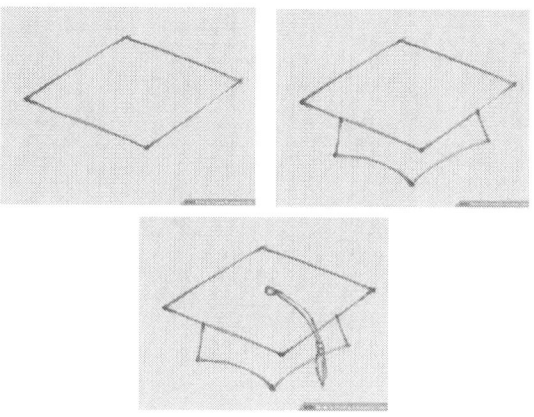

4: Paint them a picture

Drawing models

Matt Church, as I have noted, first taught me the importance of visual communication. Here I'll share what I learned from Matt. I can't do justice to Matt's teachings at Thought Leaders Business School here, but I don't have to. If what follows sufficiently whets your appetite to know more about model building, I encourage you to visit https://www.mattchurch.com/pinksheetprocess to learn from the expert. Matt's pink sheet process for capturing your intellectual property, including the use of models, is pure genius!

The building blocks

There are four key building blocks for drawing a model: a circle, a triangle, a rectangle and a line. With these you can depict any concept or vision of the future you want to.

There are also four categories of models, which are the four quadrants of Dr Bernice McCarthy's 4MAT model: *Why, What, How* and *If.*

Why models cover the 'what's in it for me?' question you need to answer for anyone you need to persuade. *What* models cover the key concepts you are trying to articulate. *How* models let you to show how you are going to achieve the outcomes you are advising are attainable. *If* models invite the person you are conversing with to consider other alternatives, to explore your advice in a collaborative manner.

Figure 4.9: The 4MAT Model

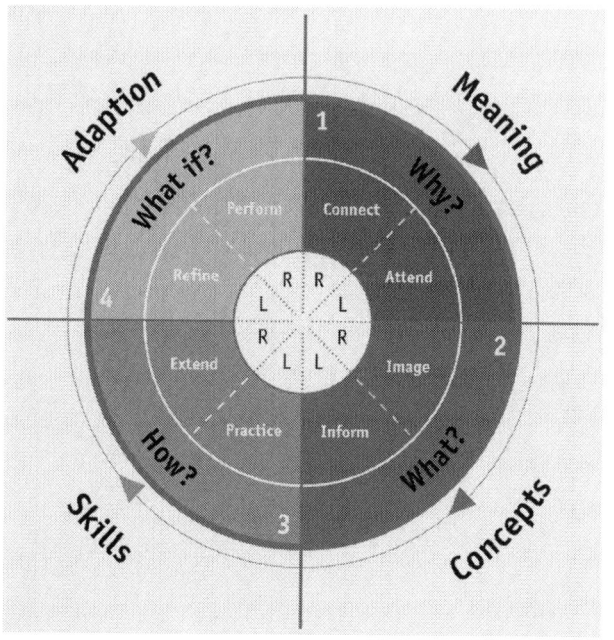

Source: 4mat.eu[18]

Let me take you through each one in turn.

Why models

There are two typical types of why models. The first is the ladder model (Figure 4.10). In the concept column the why model is helping your audience to see where they are and where they could be in relation to the concept. If the concept is around

4: Paint them a picture

leadership, the worst place might be *Tyrant* or *Autocrat*, whereas at the top of the ladder might be *Inspirational*. The second column is used to explain what they have where they are and what they might gain by moving up the ladder. For example, being seen as a poor leader is likely to mean you have trouble effecting change. So the positive rung could be *Inspiring* and the very positive rung could be *Transformational*. Figure 1.3 in chapter 1 is an example of the ladder model.

Figure 4.10: Ladder why model

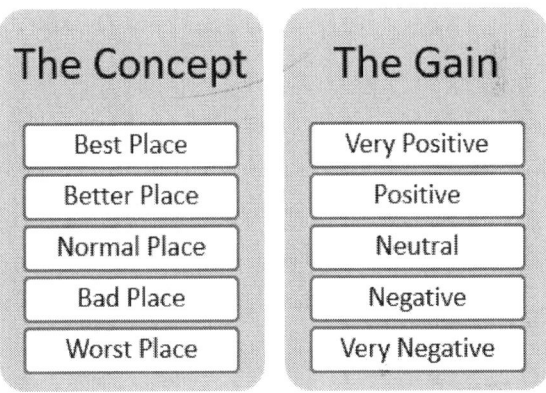

The other key why model type is the S-curve. Figure 4.11 depicts a very simple version. The S-curve shows a tough start, with a rapid advance in the middle and the need to push hard to get home. In the construction industry, for instance, the S-curve shows how plenty of effort and cost go into sinking the foundations, with little to show for it. When the main frame of the structure is being built, the progress is far more evident and compares well to the effort and cost. However, the final fit-out has many challenges and can be plagued by expensive glitches. The 'defects period' on a build can be very painful for both builder and client, with lots of effort and cost for very little gain, especially for the builder.

You can do much more with S-curves, for example by giving them x and y axes with labels. You will see an example in the practical examples section at the end of this book.

Figure 4.11: The S-curve

What models

What models provide detail. They give you the opportunity to show your depth of understanding (see the first example in Figure 4.12). I use this model to explain how any implementation of policy, process or system comes up against politics, culture and capability. It allows me to talk about the impact of each and what needs to be considered in design and implementation, so I help produce blue ribbon and not red tape. The model helps people remember my views — and hopefully appreciate how knowledgeable I am.

Figure 4.12: Sample what model for an organisation

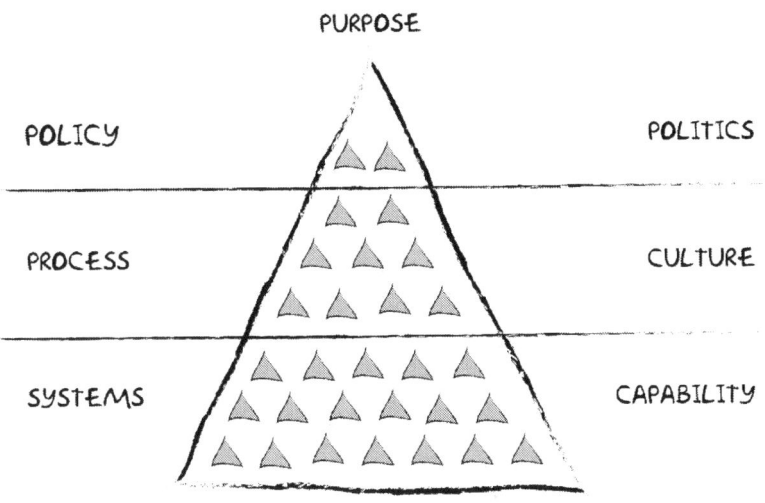

The second example (Figure 4.13) depicts magnets and imaginary magnetic fields. It is still a what model as it helps me explain what is going on as senior management try to disseminate information to the extremities of the organisation, where in turn people are trying to get information to senior management. A magnetic repulsion effect is created and information flow is blocked.

Figure 4.13: Sample what model for organisational knowledge management

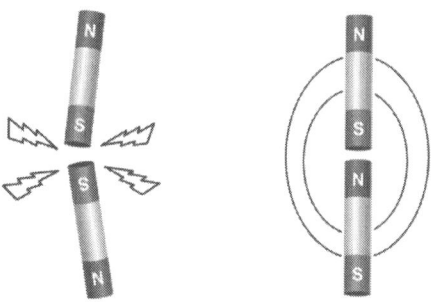

How models

How models are my favourite. You will see many examples throughout this book. The classic how model is the Venn diagram, conceived by English mathematician John Venn, who published his first diagrams in 1880.[19] Venn used his diagrams to illustrate the common elements of two or three different things. Figure 4.14 uses a Venn diagram to show how errors occur when the 'blind spots' caused by our psychological biases obstruct our clear thinking.

Figure 4.14: Sample Venn diagram

4: Paint them a picture

The Venn can be used in so many ways. Figure 4.15 is one of my personal favourites, as it explains so much about life. I call it 'the story of you' because it shows how we are each a product of our genes, our environment and the values we choose to live by. The intersections of the three circles help me to understand people at another level. I hope this diagram and the many others in this book inspire you to explore Venns.

Figure 4.15: The story of you

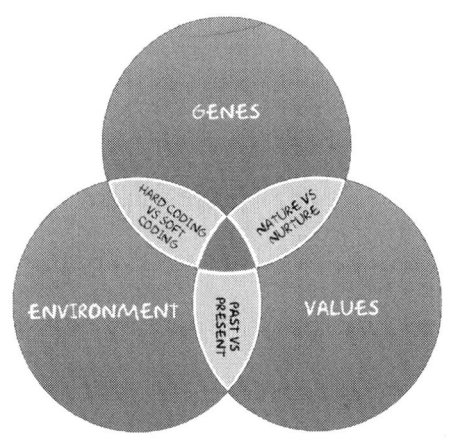

What if models

Why models explain where people are and where they could be, in the sense of climbing from a bad place to a much better place. What if models illustrate the difference between the here and now and where you want to be, and help describe how to get there. Let me explain.

My favourite what if example is my Performance Diagnostic Model (Figure 4.16). Here I must give credit to my colleague Paul Guignard, of The Capability Institute, whose inspiring views on what creates and drives performance led to the model's creation. In essence, it can be summed up like this: if a bunch of six-year-olds are running your organisation you'll have a fun, open culture, but a knowledge gap, whereas if you have a bunch of PhDs with a very poor culture running your organisation you are likely to have a knowledge block. They simply won't be heard or will be shut down.

I use the model to help determine if the performance issue is capability or culture, or both! From there we move on to discussions about the level of proactive leadership or the type of change agents needed to improve performance.

Figure 4.16: Performance Diagnostic Model

Drawing conclusions

I hope you have drawn the conclusion that there is something in this drawing aspect to building your influence with your staff and stakeholders. If you haven't, check out the resources listed after the chapter summary. If I haven't convinced you, I hope they can.

Chapter summary

To be honest, I fought the urge to draw for a long time because I thought I was so bad at it. In truth, I am. Just take a look at the hand-drawn figures in this book. My hope is that this chapter has impressed on you that *no matter what your drawing ability*, you can draw. More importantly, drawing will:

- help people understand you and your advice
- rectify any mistaken mental images they may have
- create powerful emotions to influence their decision making
- give their memory 'something to hang their hat on'.

Combined, these are very powerful reasons to step up, grab the whiteboard marker and start to draw in your very next meeting.

Recommended resources

Matt Church, Pink Sheet Process. www.mattchurch.com/pinksheetprocess

Dan Roam (2013). *The Back of the Napkin: Solving problems and selling ideas with pictures*, Portfolio.

Graham Shaw (2015). 'Why people believe they can't draw — and how to prove they can'. TEDxHull.20

5

Tell them a story

Emotional stuff

I know several very good storytellers, including my mum. I also know a couple of people who have written great books on storytelling and who train people in this noble art. The lesser known is Patricia McMillan, author of *Make IT Matter: The surprising secret for leading digital transformation*. The better known is Gabrielle Dolan, who co-authored *Hooked*, wrote *Storytelling for Job Interviews* and had a bestseller with her most recent book, *Stories for Work: The essential guide to business storytelling*.

When I first met Dolan and McMillan and found out they made a living through teaching people about storytelling, my initial reaction was 'WTF! People buy that stuff?'

Oh, how wrong we can be! What I didn't recognise was that I was already using storytelling in my busy little consulting practice, and I had completely missed both how effective it had been for me and how much *more* effective it could be. All I needed was to become proactive and consciously build it into what I do.

The oldest story I use in my consulting practice is about being a chemical engineer, how successful my profession proved to be at creating major industrial and environmental catastrophes, and how we as an industry had to change or be regulated into an isolated corner. I give examples of the mini-catastrophes I have seen or researched in depth. Without really thinking about it, I was already using stories about the industry from which my career had sprung to engage people, to give them some background on me and to instil in them a sense of urgency, or at least a sense that change was needed.

What was reinforced for me by both Dolan and McMillan was that storytelling is about creating emotions in people. And, as I have already argued, **triggering emotion in people is critical if you wish to persuade them.** Dolan quotes a study of over 1,400 marketing campaigns by the Institute of Practitioners in Advertising (IPA) in the UK. It found that marketing campaigns that used emotion only were about 32 per cent effective whereas those that used logic only were a dismal 16 per cent effective.[21] It is no wonder we feel frustrated when we give someone all the pertinent facts only for them to choose the wrong path because of their emotional bias.

What of emotion combined with logic? According to Dolan, the IPA study found that when logic and emotion were combined in campaigns they were 26 per cent effective. That's right. Less effective than emotion only! If you think about it, we see this happen all the time. Here's a list of decisions people make that are irrational but that they justify to themselves because they really, really want to believe it. They are emotionally tied up in it.

- Gamblers believe they can beat the house at the roulette wheel in a casino.
- People will vote for a political party because they have always voted for that side of politics, even though the party's current policies will be detrimental to them.
- Many climbers have died on Mount Everest because they pushed on to the summit when they were past the 'must turn back' cut-off time they had set themselves before they left. The summit was in sight — it seemed so attainable.
- Entrepreneurs will sink more and more cash into their 'baby' even though to anyone else the scheme is dead in the water.
- Parents refuse to believe, against the evidence, that their child did anything wrong.

Emotions are powerful, and to be a good persuader you need to be able to create and harness them in others.

Before I go on, I want to return to the Institute of Practitioners in Advertising's finding that applying logic actually reduced the success of campaigns. To a logic guy like me, the thought that using logic to help persuade people is counterproductive doesn't sit comfortably. And with good reason. We're playing a long game: we're advisers, not door-to-door salespeople. People need to be able to trust our advice. If we rely only on emotion, defying logic, eventually our advice will come unstuck and we will have destroyed trust. And trust is a very precious commodity.

The Pathfinder Model is a subtle blend of logic and emotion, with logic packaged and presented to create and harness a desired emotion in those you wish to persuade.

Connect what?

The Pathfinder Model encourages you to 'tell them a story to connect'. To connect them to you and, whenever possible, to connect them to your advice — that is, to make them feel good about both you and your advice. If you don't feel you can achieve both at once, then choose one. Here are some thoughts to help you to choose the story that best suits a particular situation.

The Story Ladder

When choosing a story, consider how telling it will help your audience to connect with you. It could be a highly emotional and sad story that draws their sympathy: they feel your pain and have an urge to hug you or give you a helping hand. It could be a story that simply makes them laugh and feel good. Both could influence them to like you, which, as Dale Carnegie established back in the 1930s, is an essential element for improving your ability to influence.[22]

Table 5.1 lists six types of stories you can tell, three of them positive and three negative. When you are choosing a story to tell for the first time or to a new audience, stop and ask yourself which category it fits into. If you find it is below the line you are likely to damage your ability to influence by using it; if above the line, you are likely to improve your ability to influence. It is not always possible or desirable to find a story in the top category, LOVE, so don't get hung up on it. **Just make sure your story will have a positive effect, then rely on the other elements of the Pathfinder Model to do their stuff.**

Table 5.1: The Story Ladder

Effect of story	Type of story
LOVE for you	You made them want to follow you.
ADMIRE you	You inspired them.
LIKE you	You entertained them or made them feel good about themselves.
JEALOUS of you	You positioned yourself as the hero or you succeeded when they failed.
DISLIKE you	You chose a story that is not interesting to them or is not what they are about.
DISDAIN for you	You provoked them to anger. You could not have picked a worse story.

The Story Impact Wheel

Now things get really interesting. The Story Impact Wheel (Figure 5.1) helps you to think about the potential effect on your audience of the story you have in mind and to find a story best suited to the type of effect you want in a given situation. Let me explain.

5: Tell them a story

The wheel helps you to choose a type of story based on two dimensions: *Personal vs Non-personal* and *Emotional vs Surprising.* When combined, the impact can be expressed as Feel, Think, Like or Love.

Figure 5.1: The Story Impact Wheel

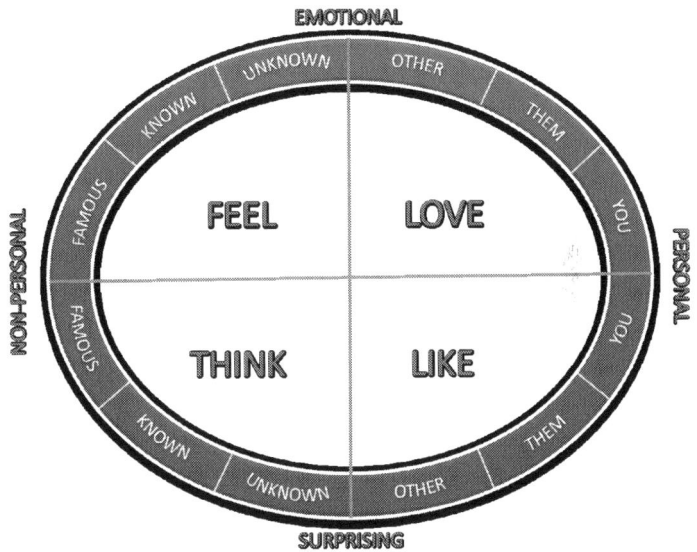

Personal vs Non-personal

A story needs a main character, right? Well, that main character could be you, someone you know personally or your audience. Otherwise it is non-personal, and for good reason, as I will explain.

Personal stories can have the greatest impact because they are directly relatable. While getting people to *feel* and *think* by telling them a personal story, you are also likely to incline them to *like* you, and maybe even feel a bit of '*love*' for you. Stories about you can be great, but make sure you check where they fit on the Story Ladder before using them. Stories about people known personally to you and your audience are often powerful because of the intimate knowledge you share.

When my son Doug was considering his next move with his university studies I told him a story about a friend of mine, Hook, whom Doug knows well. Hook once told me that his epiphany came one day when he looked around and saw that all of our group had graduated except him. He was working in a job that did not enthral him, with a couple of failed attempts at university already behind him. For the next couple of years he disappeared socially while he knuckled down and completed his degree. Doug could relate to this story very well. He said, 'Yeah, some of my mates are graduating right now.'

While personal stories can be the most effective, non-personal stories may be your best choice if you want it to be 'not about them or you'. Or perhaps the story is simply perfect for the situation. The impact wheel breaks down the types of people the story could be about into those who are genuinely *famous* (Oprah Winfrey, say), someone *known* to you both (an influential CEO in your industry, for example), or someone *unknown* to your audience. Each subject can be effective. Famous may have an advantage if your audience particularly admires or detests them!

5: Tell them a story

Emotional vs Surprising

As well as a main character, every story turns on an event or incident — something must happen. **Stories with the greatest impact tell of an event that is emotional or surprising or both.** Above I gave some statistics on the impact of emotion on decision making. Triggering an emotional response is king. A surprise, however, can stir up a range of other emotions, from inspiration to happiness, which can also have an impact.

A word of caution here. Check the Story Ladder before you use an emotional or surprising story. Not all emotions are desirable, and not all surprises are good ones!

Now you understand the two dimensions of the Story Impact Wheel, let me explain how these dimensions combine into one of the four quadrants of Feel, Think, Like or Love to help you identify the right type of story for a given situation. Perhaps you don't yet have a story that fits and have to go find one. At least you know what you are looking for now.

Feel

Stories in this quadrant are used to stir emotion in your audience in relation to the decision you want them to make. For example, telling a story that is not widely known about someone famous who once had an addiction can create awareness of susceptibility to addiction or an understanding that the condition is surprisingly common and the affected individuals should not be condemned.

Think

Sometimes you need someone to think more deeply about an issue. Perhaps they are avoiding it and you simply have not been able to get their attention. An excellent way to do so is to surprise them. Surprise prompts the brain to think about and analyse the situation. By looking further at an issue, your audience will begin to see possibilities other than the one they were fixated on.

I use a story about Australian skier and Winter Olympics gold medallist Alisa Camplin, whom I had the pleasure of hearing speak at a conference. She recalled being introduced to the 'risk matrix' in a meeting when she worked at IBM. Using this concept in her training regime meant planning for every contingency so she could handle anything that might go wrong on the day. She referred to it as 'gold' and the secret to her gold medal success.

No one would have expected such an idea to lie at the heart of Camplin's performance success. Her story gets my audience thinking about 'risk management done well'. It also lets them know that I empathise with businesspeople who have been impacted negatively by well-meaning risk managers.

Like

Creating a surprise is good. A humorous one is even better. In fact, surprise is what humour is all about. We laugh because of the unexpected path we are taken down. No one laughs at a joke they can see coming from a mile away.

A word of caution here. We all have a funny story to share, but the story must be relevant. Sometimes a speaker will start with an unrelated joke. It may make them more likeable, and people may be more willing to listen, but they have missed the opportunity to draw their audience's attention to the topic. The problem can escalate if you use a non-relevant funny story in a meeting. If your audience is not up for small talk, you risk merely irritating them.

I added a new funny story to my repertoire recently. It is about my insane proclivity for failing to notice the bleeding obvious. I was attending a program put on by Dan Gregory and Kieran Flanagan at the Impossible Institute. During the session I noticed Dan's fantastic library. Many of the books I had read, many I wanted to read. I kept getting distracted as I tried to read the spines from a distance. Here's the funny thing: the books were not randomly placed or filed alphabetically by author or title; they were colour-coded. Books with covers of similar colours were placed together, and I didn't notice it until it was time to go. Everyone had a good laugh at my expense.

I use that story when I want to talk about insight vs observation. While my lack of observation often leads to embarrassment (I have many other funny stories I can use!), this lack often allows me to find insights others can't. I seem to filter out what I deem unimportant in order to get to the real issue. At least that's my defence, and I'm sticking to it!

Love

Everyone wants to be loved. If you can share a personal story with your audience, you will likely create strong and positive emotions — you are creating L O V E!

One story I use when I run my Winning Conversations Program makes an immense impact and wins me a whole lot of love. It's about my daughter's mission to convince my wife and me to get a dog, and it shows how even a child can use stories effectively to get what they want.

Now isn't that the perfect segue into the next section?

Even *you* can tell stories

I get the same questions over and over and over: 'What if I am just not a storyteller? Don't you agree that most people in my role are introverts? We aren't "salesy" people, and we're not storytellers.' And I always give the same answer:

Everyone is a storyteller. Everyone.

Have you never recounted something that happened in your life? Have you never had someone sitting with you at home or at work listening to you recount that event and asking you questions about it? Yes, you have. We all have. And their asking questions *proves* they were engaged.

So you *can* tell stories, and here's how.

Storytelling guide

What makes a great storyteller? The best storytellers remember the detail. Each story has little particulars that embellish the story in a small but telling way. They see the colour in their stories. Every story is colourful to them; nothing is drab or boring. And they have a clever turn of phrase. They don't just say,

5: Tell them a story

'... and then she fell over.' They say, '... and then she fell and landed right on her derrière!'

We have already established that you can tell stories, but you might still doubt that you can be a great storyteller. I believe you can. Here's how.

Construct of a story

What does a story consist of? Most often the stories we remember from our childhood and teen years have heroes and villains, or at least challenges. There is a start, a 'journey' and a sad or happy ending. Okay, occasionally some artistic type likes to leave you with an unresolved ending. Not my cup of tea, and certainly not one I would recommend if you wish to influence someone. For the purpose of creating your stories of influence, let's keep it very simple. Here is what a story consists of:

1. A character: Characters can be people (real or imagined), animals or objects (for example, the story of a tree that grows from a seedling, produces food for the forest animals and eventually dies). Multiple characters can make the story more entertaining or powerful. Too many can get confusing.
2. An incident: Something must happen. A good story often has plenty of sub-incidents that you can choose to bring in or leave out.
3. A point: Every story must have a point to it — or rather, you use it to make a point to your audience. Most stories can be used to make more than one point, but don't try to make too many!

How do you construct your stories and get them match fit for the game of influencing? The next section will guide you.

Ten Step Guide

1. Collate

You have lots of stories. You just need to bring them all to mind, collate them and store them in one place. I store mine in Evernote, tagged as 'story'. Table 5.2 below will help you to compile yours. As a strong memory comes to mind, write just a few words about it. For all your personal stories you can move on to step 2. For your non-personal stories, you will need to do some research about a well-known figure to find a great story about them, assuming you don't already know one. Ultimately you will have a long list of potential stories. You need only one good story to get you going, but if you can find the time now you should work up about a dozen to give you a broad base from which you can select to suit any influencing situation.

Table 5.2: Story collation

Place to look	Thought provokers
Childhood years	Best friend, favourite place, pets, the naughty corner, holidays, notable teachers
Teenage years	Friendship group, notable teachers, holidays, achievements (academic, arts, sport), hospital time
College/university	Friends, lecturers, projects, part-time work, road trips
Travel	Locations, companions, romance, friendly locals, hardship, culture shock

5: Tell them a story

Place to look	Thought provokers
Work	First job, worst job, best job, favourite colleague, least favourite colleague, hardest day, biggest day
Sports	Triumphs and tragedies, freakiest event
Hobbies (art, music, science, nature)	Collections, clubs/companions, equipment, lessons, best days, worst days
Holidays	Top three, worst three, cheapest, most expensive, closest, longest
Famous people	Politicians, actors, businesspeople, sport, literature, historical
Best days ever	Love, heroism, clever, reward, award
Worst days ever	Love, death, injury, embarrassment
Weirdest experience	Person, animal, machine, job, food

2. Characterise

Write down the main character and any supporting characters for each story. Add a few points about them that provide you with material to embellish the story and give it colour. Perhaps note what they were wearing, what they were doing, where they were or where they were going.

3. Analyse

Set down the main incident, any key ancillary incidents and a few points about each.

4. Conceptualise

For each story, think about concepts you might be able to link it to. For example, my story about my daughter giving me Reinbeers for Christmas could be linked to ideas around simple gift giving, ingenuity, resourcefulness and many more. Write down a few for each of your stories.

5. Compose

Now it's time to compose your story. While you need not actually write up three-minute, one-minute and 30-second versions, keep in mind that in some circumstances you may need to leave out much of the detail to make your point quickly and concisely. One trick is to first write up the 30-second version and then embellish the story to give it some colour, for example adding more detail about characters or the incident. You could use a metaphor or analogy — feel free to use a thesaurus to find new ways of expressing a point.

Once you have finished, put it aside for a few days then review it cold to see how it strikes you then. My father-in-law was in advertising well before the days of personal computers. He would often write a piece and mail it to himself. While in the post it was out of sight, out of mind.

6. Stand

Okay, you have stories and ideas of what you could link them to. Now it's time to identify your audience and pick a story for them. First you need to stand in their shoes so you have a good understanding of them. Then use the Story Impact Wheel.

7. Impact

Based on your analysis of your audience and how you want to influence them, decide what impact you are aiming for.

For example, if the person is a senior executive in another business unit, you may want to get them to *feel* differently about your project. Maybe their blinkered view blinds them to the possibilities, so you want to get them to *think* differently. Perhaps you got off to a poor start with them, and you want to persuade them to *like* you and your project. Or maybe, given how important your project is to you and the organisation, it is going to take such a leap of faith for this executive to buy in that you need to find some *love*.

8. Select

Now select a story from those you have collated. If, for example, you want the executive to *think* differently about the project, you need to surprise them into a different thought pattern. You could use a personal story or one about a well-known person.

In my first book, *DECIDE*, I wanted to make a point about working hard and smart versus just working hard or avoiding the hard work altogether. I found a story about Mark Twain and the Linotype machine, invented, not by Twain, in the late 19th century to mass produce newspapers. (The Linotype machine was still producing the New York Times until 1978, almost a century later.) In the story Twain invests in a similar machine, James Paige's Paige Compositor. They came second in the race to invent a mass-producing machine and this was a major contributor to, if not the cause of Twain's bankruptcy. Both Paige and the successful inventor, Ottmar Mergenthaler, worked hard, but Mergenthaler worked smarter and designed a machine that was cheaper and more reliable and was in the market three years earlier than Paige's. Paige was guilty of trying to create the perfect machine, which resulted in his machine having 18,000 parts and being markedly more expensive! I now use the story to impress on internal advisers that the secret to blue ribbon is simplicity in design.

In my experience, if you look for stories in your fields of interest you will more easily find something you can use to make a person *feel* or *think* differently. You will enjoy the process of discovering the story and enjoy it even more when you use it. Because you are able to share that joy, you will also draw people to *like* or maybe even *love* you and want to follow in your footsteps.

9. Check

Check you have not picked the wrong story, and that you are above the line on the Story Ladder.

10. Practise

The more you practise your stories, the better you will get at delivering them. You can practise by yourself in front of a mirror. Better still, practise on friends and colleagues.

What should be the focus of your practice? This story should help guide you.

US actor John Lithgow, who played lead roles in movies such as *The World According to Garp* and the TV series *3rd Rock from the Sun* and *The Crown*, was being interviewed on US TV station

5: Tell them a story

CBS about his new play, *Stories by Heart*. In the play he reads and acts out stories from the book of the same name. In fact, it is the same book from which his father read him bedtime stories. During the interview he is asked about his ability to make different sounds with his mouth. They cut to a scene of him acting as a barber giving a haircut. Then, live, he makes the sounds of cuts and snips of the scissors. Very realistic.

'The whole evening is about imagination,' Lithgow explains. 'Not so much mine. It's the imagination of the audience. My challenge is to create a world, right up there on stage, to make everybody see things that aren't there. To make everyone see the difference between one, two, three, four, five characters on stage at the same time, including a parrot [smiles and pokes his tongue out to form a beak].'[23]

Lithgow is saying you should focus your practice on your delivery. Deliver with maximum effect. What physical movements can you make? What props can you use? What sounds can you generate? What accents can you assume? What can you do to make the story come alive?

An escape capsule

Despite everything you have read about storytelling, you may still be a little hesitant about telling stories in some situations. I get that. So here is your own escape capsule.

The Storytelling Escape Capsule (Figure 5.2) is a variation on one drawn by my friend Donna McGeorge in her Engaging Training program. Her diagram aimed to help you identify when you should or should not be in front of the room when training a group of people. My adaptation aims to help you decide when to tell stories, when to have someone else have the conversation or make the presentation, and when to use an alternative to a full-blown story. It is pretty self-explanatory.

1. If you know your audience well and you know your topic well, go for it. Tell a story.
2. If you don't know your audience or topic well, you are not the right person for the job. Find someone who is. Have them use the Pathfinder Model to help them understand the audience. Help them design the picture they are going to draw, choose and develop the right story, and be ready to demonstrate credibility. Help them give it their best shot.
3. If you know your audience well and they are familiar with you, but you have limited knowledge of the topic, use examples. With examples you get to explore the topic with your audience and co-create a solution. You are conceding you don't know the right answer. After all, how could you if you have just admitted you are not particularly knowledgeable about the topic?
4. If you know your topic well but you are not experienced in working with your audience, use analogies. For example, if presenting to the executive for the first time, you and/or they may feel a story is not appropriate. An analogy, with an illuminating twist, will often work better.

5: Tell them a story

Figure 5.2: Storytelling Escape Capsule

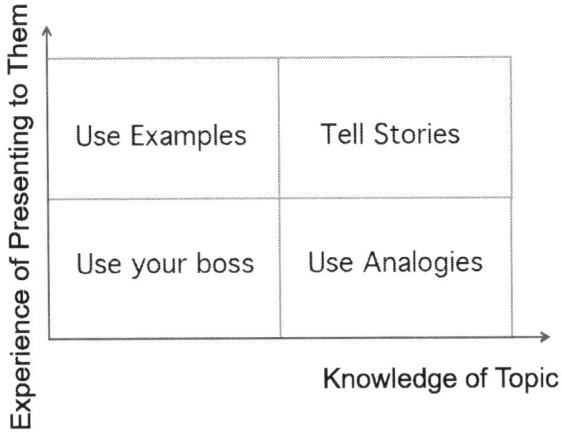

Here is an example of a 'story' I tell that uses both an analogy and an example.

When I describe a challenge that is going to start difficult, get some rapid traction, meet some bumps on the road and then require a final push to embed the benefits achieved, I compare it to growing a small start-up into a big business. Using an S-curve diagram I explain that a typical small business is hard to get off the ground but grows quite quickly at some point before it plateaus for a while during the consolidation period. You get some processes and systems in place, then move out of home or the garage into offices or a manufacturing facility. More growth is usually followed by another plateau when you take on more staff or expand the operation. Later you may consolidate in one market while launching in another or introducing a new product line.

Then I ask for a great example of the kind of trajectory I have just described. I don't wait long for an answer, though, as I want to push on to give them an example pretty much everyone on Earth can recognise: Microsoft. It started in a garage and it grew, with some hiccoughs along the way (plateaus and troughs), to become one of the biggest companies in the world.

This 'story' of mine, then, is part analogy, part example, and the example has a well-known story behind it. If I want to, I can bring out more and more about Bill Gates and the history of Microsoft. The more I do, the more it becomes a full-fledged story.

So if you don't feel comfortable telling a full story, work on analogies and examples your audience can easily relate to. And as your confidence grows, build your analogies into stories.

Chapter summary

I started this chapter by emphasising the important role of emotions in decision making and the impact stories have on emotions. I did my best to convince you that everyone, including *you*, can tell a story.

I also provided you with a range of tools to help you identify stories to tell, whether personal or research based. And I got you thinking about emotional versus surprising stories and how by choosing well you can make people *feel, think, like* or *love*.

Next I introduced a methodology for building an idea for a story into a full-blown story with three-minute, one-minute and 30-second versions.

Finally, I suggested an escape capsule for those still lacking in confidence as storytellers. The trick is to start with an analogy or metaphor, and slowly build it into a story with characters and embellishing details.

Storytelling works by engaging an audience and driving emotion. When you watch the faces of people listening to a story, you can see clearly how engaged with the storyteller they become. Next you need to *make them believe*.

Recommended resources

Andrew Stanton (2012). 'The Clues to a Great Story', TED Talk.

Patricia MacMillan (2016). *Make IT Matter: The surprising secret for leading digital transformation.* Wiley.

Gabrielle Dolan (2017). *Stories for Work: The essential guide to business storytelling.* Wiley.

Dr Mardy Grothe (2008). *I Never Met a Metaphor I Didn't Like: A comprehensive compilation of history's greatest analogies, metaphors, and similes*, Harper.

6

Make them believe

Incredibility

Credibility is the final piece of the Pathfinder Model puzzle that will make you incredible at persuading people your advice is right for them.

We all want to be credible, especially when we are giving advice. It hurts not to be taken seriously. Sometimes we will be giving advice to people who are close to us or who know us well. The level of credibility we establish with them over time will be increased or diminished by our next piece of advice. Hence the adage, 'You are only as good as your last job.' For those we aren't close to, we need to establish our credibility. Quickly.

What makes someone credible? This is a question I ask in my Winning Conversations Program. We workshop it. Experience, honesty, composure, integrity, knowledge, charisma, authenticity and intelligence are all common responses. I boil them all down to just three attributes that capture the essence of credibility: *trustworthiness, adaptability* and *expertise*.

6: Make them believe

Figure 6.1: The three main attributes of credibility

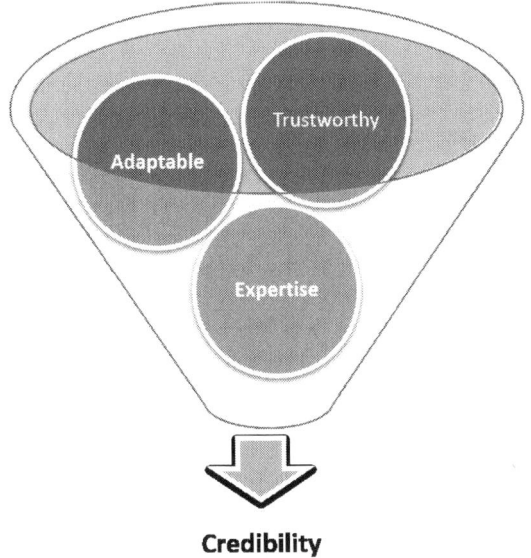

Trustworthiness

Being trustworthy is essential for credibility. Have you ever worked in an organisation where management wasn't honest with you? What level of respect did you have for them? It might have been an acceptable level while things were going well, but when the going got tough I'll bet the knives were out.

When having an influencing conversation with someone, trustworthiness connotes more than just honesty. First there's integrity and authenticity. If you change your views to suit your current needs, you are seen as lacking integrity or as fake. If you stick to your values, you demonstrate your integrity and authenticity and are seen as trustworthy. Changing your view for legitimate reasons, and explaining this change, builds trust.

Then there is fairness and unselfishness. Those who treat people equitably hold the moral high ground, above those who play favourites or give way to their personal biases. If you give credit where credit is due, you build trust in spades. Never steal another person's thunder!

Finally there is the ability to give bad news. To build the highest level of trust, you will need to be able to tell the hard truths. In Part III I'll give you a tried-and-tested methodology for giving bad news.

Adaptability

When you first encounter it, you may struggle with this idea as an element of credibility. **Answer this: What has adaptability done for every surviving species on the planet, and why are Elon Musk, CEO of SpaceX, and others looking to the stars? It's about surviving and thriving. You cannot be credible if you don't adapt and are no longer around.**

I hope I have already persuaded you that when it comes to influencing you have to stand in your audience's shoes, feel what they are feeling and act accordingly. You have to be sensitive and empathetic. If you are adaptable you can respect the formalities of the boardroom *and* the informalities of the shop floor. Adaptability allows you to listen better. If you feel comfortable in every environment, you will naturally adapt your tone, language and body language to suit your audience.

You may think you're already an adaptable person. Find out what others think, though. Pick some work colleagues and some people close to you and ask them to identify one or two people they would describe as adaptable. Then ask them how you might rate compared to those people.

If you know you are not adaptable, or if you discover that others think you are not, you will need to make a conscious effort to work on this. Remember, it is not about flip-flopping. It is about a willingness to listen and to be sensitive and empathetic.

Expertise

I'm sure you are an expert in your chosen field. That's one reason you have had the level of success you have in influencing people. However, there is expertise and there is expertise. First, you need skills and knowledge. Second, you need to be able to apply them competently in a range of circumstances. And third, you need a track record of doing so. There is nothing quite like recognised qualifications, years of experience and a raft of successes behind you to maximise your ability to influence.

The fourth component of expertise is understanding what you don't know, being transparent about the limitations of your expertise and asking the right questions. You don't want to be known as someone who sees every problem in the same way. You don't want to be seen as a hammer for whom everything looks like a nail.

Let's explore how you can develop your credibility, then we will look at how you can put all your good work together to have a credible conversation. A winning conversation.

Developing credibility

You know you have developed credibility with many people over your lifetime. You probably haven't given all that much thought to exactly how you have done it, you just have. Given you are reading this book, you are evidently determined to influence even more effectively and to take on new influencing challenges. While the *stand*, *paint* and *tell* of the Pathfinder Model will have given you plenty of ammunition, you cannot rest on your laurels when it comes to building your credibility.

Developing trust

Trust takes many forms. Trusting someone to do the right thing by you, trusting their judgement and trusting them to deliver are examples. Trust is something that is developed over time and can be lost in an instant. You need to think of both the long and the short term.

Trust is determined by your behaviour. Your choices. First you need to overcome the lure of short-term gain. To do so you need a good picture of the long term, of who you will be and how others will view you. Try this exercise.

Write down five words that describe your own personal values. Here are mine:

6: Make them believe

- loving
- caring
- fair
- resourceful
- optimistic

Now stop and think about what your family, friends and work colleagues might think your values are. What has been your track record over the short, medium and long term?

Developing adaptability

I've said that adaptability is about both the capacity for long-term survival and the ability to stand in someone else's shoes. Interestingly, the processes of building both are intertwined.

The secret is to develop a growth mindset and to be creative in your thinking. With a growth mindset you are inherently better able to adapt to changes in your physical, team and corporate environment. You look on hardship as a learning challenge rather than a roadblock. And being creative gives you two important skills — first, to be creative in standing in your audience's shoes, and second to find creative solutions to their problems. Let's tackle the growth mindset first.

With a fixed mindset you believe you are limited and can't improve. A growth mindset motivates you to keep improving, to try things out even if you are likely to fail because you know you will learn from the experience. In her book *Mindset: The New Psychology of Success*, Dr Carol Dweck reports on her years of research into motivation and shifting people from a fixed to a growth mindset.

From working with children, Dweck and her colleagues worked out that they could shift children from fixed to growth mindset by praising their efforts, rather than their results. 'Effort' can apply to many things, from a strategy employed to perseverance with a challenge. Based on her research, much has been accomplished in the field of business performance management over the past ten years.

I recommend you do two things. First, read Dweck's book or at least watch her TED Talk. Second, create a reward system for yourself that encourages you to try new things. I'll leave to you what the rewards might be. Here are some examples of activities you could pursue to build your adaptability:

- Read a business book to open your mind — maybe a controversial one in your field.
- Sign up to a podcast that interests you and listen to the entire series.
- Read five business articles on one subject to appreciate how views differ.
- Make a presentation to a group *and* ask for hard-hitting feedback.
- Draw something, anything, to present in your next three business meetings.
- Tell a story to a family member or friend to make a point.
- Tell a story at work to make a point.

6: Make them believe

Repeat and repeat the exercise until it becomes habit, and you will find yourself permanently in a growth mindset. Happy days!

What about being creative? Creativity can be learned too. Begin by reading about it. I recommend Edward De Bono's *Lateral Thinking*. He has written some sixty books on the topic of thinking and creativity! Or Google creative or lateral thinking. Then test at least one — or better still, three — of the creative techniques you have read about. Trust me on this. You will get better at coming up with creative ideas and helping others to do the same.

Let me finish with an illustration of a combination of growth mindset, creative thinking and standing in their shoes to gain an advantage.

An ABC Radio National *Sum of All Parts* podcast, 'Shoal Attack! A school of fish help the Australian netball team win a gold medal',[24] describes how a scientist studied the behaviour of schools of fish and used his findings to analyse the collective behaviour of opposition netball teams. Applying this research, the Australian team designed tactics to counter the plays, gaining an advantage by forcing errors from their opponents. A mighty big advantage, as it turned out. This is a great listen for anyone thinking about collective behaviour within their organisation.

Developing expertise

The ultimate test of your expertise is to use it to deliver wise advice. It is one thing to be an expert. It is another thing for people to value and seek out your counsel. The Pathfinder Model is designed to help you get there. **No matter what picture you paint or what story you tell, you need to make sure your specific advice is as good as it can possibly be.**

Test yourself now with reference to the last piece of advice you provided to someone. Where was it on the scale from relevant through to true wisdom?

To develop your expertise to the extent that you can consistently deliver wisdom when advising someone on a decision obviously takes a lot of work and, yes, experience. However, there are things you can do in the short and medium term to develop your expertise.

Developing a growth mindset, reading business books and articles, and listening to podcasts will help. So will using

Google to research topics. There are, of course, more traditional education avenues such as studying for a degree or diploma. Formal study is a different proposition today than it was even ten years ago. Now you can study online, and even for free if you don't want the accreditation. Yep, online and free. Say you want to develop expertise in machine learning. You can take a free course through the world-renowned Stanford University, though you will miss out on some of the assignments, and if you want a certificate to say you completed the course you will need to pay.

With a growth mindset and all the learning resources now available, there is no excuse for not building your expertise over time.

Instant credibility

Instant credibility is important when you are influencing someone you don't know well or whom you may never have met. There are two key pathways to gaining instant credibility with these people: one is to have a credible third person recommend you; the second is about how you show up to your first meeting with them. I won't to go into how to arrange a recommendation or referral, other than to say that sometimes if you don't ask you won't get. I will spend a little time on how you show up.

Nick Cave and I have something in common. We both fell in love at first sight. In 'First impressions — the face bias'[25] on Radio National's *All in the Mind* program, Nick Cave describes seeing his future wife for the first time: everything 'came together ... in one great big crash-bang. And I was lost to her. And that was that'.

It was the lead-in to an interview by program host Lynne Malcolm of Alexander Todorov of Princeton University. Todorov is the author of *Face Value: The irresistible influence of first impressions*. Here are some fun facts from the podcast:

- We need only 200 milliseconds to form a judgement of a person.
- The happier and more rested we are, the more likely we will be seen in a positive light.
- We project how we feel — for example, power dressing for a meeting is reflected in our facial expressions.

During the interview, Malcolm referred to our programming to judge someone so quickly as 'face-ism'. Todorov explained;

> 'I often say that getting a degree in psychology is really getting a degree in modesty, because you realise that there are so many things that colour our judgements, colour our decisions, and yet we seem to be blind to these viruses. We often think that we are impervious to all kinds of effects and they only apply to other humans but not to us.'

In influencing challenges, the role of face-ism means you need to be aware that your appearance has an immediate effect on your credibility — hence the expression 'dress for success'.

Janine Garner is someone who fully gets it. In her book *It's Who You Know*, she lists ten secrets to cultivating your network to improve your connections. The first one is 'First impressions count'.

Okay, you have done all your preparation, and you are ready for a credible conversation. Wait a moment. Have you thought about the flow of the conversation? Are you going to start with a story and then paint a picture? Are you going to lay out your credentials first, or do so only if you need to? All these things matter. The next part of the book dissects the construct of a winning conversation.

Chapter summary

Belief is a choice. Those you wish to influence need to choose to believe you. While the empathy you can show from standing in their shoes, and the emotion and clarity you can create with pictures and stories, are vital, credibility wins the day. In this chapter we learned there are many personal attributes that people associate with credibility, all of which can be boiled down to just three: trust, adaptability and expertise.

Just as belief is a choice, the values you choose to live by also involve choices. If you choose unselfish values and work hard to live by them, the trust you create will reflect this.

Adaptability is important because it allows you to build the breadth and depth of your experience, as well as helping you to stand in the shoes of others. Developing your adaptability is all about a growth mindset. In this chapter I suggested a few exercises through which you can first identify how adaptable you are and then improve your adaptability.

Everyone I know would agree expertise is key to credibility. My point here is that offering good advice is not enough — you need to deliver wisdom. By standing in people's shoes you are better placed to offer them true wisdom.

Finally, people judge others on their appearance. It is in our genes. When you wish to influence I suggest you dress for success.

Recommended resources

Carol Dweck (2007). *Mindset: The new psychology of success.* Ballantine.

Carol Dweck (2014). 'The power of believing you can improve'. TED Talk.

Robert M. Krauss and Chi-Yue Chiu (2017). *Language and Social Behavior*, Columbia University and University of Hong Kong.

Jeane Fahnestock (2011). *Rhetorical Style: The uses of language in persuasion.* Oxford.

Part III

Winning Conversations

7

Construct of a conversation

A win-win in 15 minutes

It takes 8 hours to prepare about 15 minutes of advice. Those 15 minutes simply can't be wasted — hence the need for a winning conversation. How many times have you seen those 15 minutes wasted? Many, I expect. What about when the adviser had in fact understood the problem and had developed a great piece of advice? Still many, probably. What about when the adviser had all the credibility you'd think would be needed? Still many. Why? Because of all those barriers I mentioned when introducing the Pathfinder Model.

In this chapter I provide a construct for a winning conversation that takes into account all the factors that influence a conversation using the four elements of the Pathfinder Model, Stand, Tell, Paint and Make. In this example I use the four elements in sequence. In the practical examples in the following chapter, however, you will see that the sequence is not always consistent. Sometimes you may wish to lead with a story or with a picture to capture your audience's attention or to create an emotion. Sometimes you may withhold the story until near the end, to finish on a high. Or you may have a second story to make your final, clinching point. There is no right or wrong here. I encourage you to experiment as you develop your understanding of the power of the model and in this way hone your persuasive skills.

Standing in their shoes

Standing in the shoes of the person you wish to influence starts well before the conversation. It is also the beginning of the conversation, because you can't assume you have understood their situation completely. From your research and analysis, you may think you understand what makes them tick, their challenges and how they feel on certain issues, but you need to check. And check deeply.

The way you check your assumptions is by asking leading questions. Many people will tell you that the key to influencing is to ask lots of questions. In my experience, that is not always the case. If you are meeting with someone who has a negative perception of you and what you represent, they will be looking for an opportunity to shut you down. For example, an operations person meeting with someone from a support function, such as HR, procurement, risk or compliance, may hit you with, 'Don't come asking about my problems, come with solutions to them.'

In this kind of situation you need to choose your words carefully and demonstrate effort. You need to show you have done the work, you have done your best to understand their problems. Ask a leading question such as, 'I have seen … elsewhere. Is this a problem for you too?' or, 'I have seen …. elsewhere, and I'm thinking this is a problem for you as well?' If they agree they have the problem, the next step is empathy. Demonstrate that you recognise the pain this must be causing. Establish you understand their situation clearly and empathise with them. You are now ready to deliver your advice using the Paint and Tell tools and techniques of the Pathfinder Model.

If they disagree on your diagnosis of their problem, you may have got it wrong and you will need to move on to the next challenge you identified for them. If you have not in fact got it wrong, and you know it, you can do one of two things. First, you can explore it further by articulating the problem and its symptoms. This will give them the opportunity to open up because they appreciate your expertise. Or second, you can move on to other challenges you believe are related to the advice you wish to give.

If you are there to address one challenge and one challenge only, and your exploration of its symptoms leaves them in denial, then they are in the 'Unrecognised — Uncompelled' space from my Problem Compellation Model (as discussed in chapter 3), which means you need to inspire them with your Paint and Tell tools.

7: Construct of a conversation

Before I move on to the Paint, Tell and Make parts of the Pathfinder Model, I want to identify a number of issues that affect their impact on your target audience. They range from how you start the conversation to how best to deliver bad news.

First impressions

First impressions are formed by your appearance as you or they walk through the door and how you start the conversation.

We have covered the importance of physical appearance. Dress for success and you will exude confidence more naturally. When you start the conversation you want to be likeable, so a smile and a warm handshake are also key in the business environment. They need your help. You are happy to be there and are going to help them, right? Right!

Some people like small talk, others don't. The better your research of your audience, the better you will know what they prefer. I ask them how they are or make a brief comment about the weather, their office or perhaps the staff member who escorted me in. Anything to give them the opportunity to open up if they are in the mood to chat.

Deep listening

My friend Oscar Trimboli is author of *Deep Listening — Impact Beyond Words*. The book opens brilliantly with this epigraph:

> 'Every human asks to be listened to — yet what they crave most is to be heard.'

His book taught me to work on being a better listener. You may think the author of *Winning Conversations* would not need to work on listening. Well, no one is perfect, and I know I can get better at listening to my own advice in this book!

Trimboli's book opened my eyes to the impact poor listening can have on a conversation, how it can turn it into a losing conversation. Here are my key take-outs from his book:

1. *Offense.* If you give the impression you are not listening, you are likely to offend them.
2. *Empathy.* If you don't listen well, you miss out on opportunities to empathise.
3. *Confusion.* If you don't listen well, you may get the wrong end of the stick.

Be sure to listen deeply.

C-suite speak

Confusion can also result from the words you use. In 2010 I ran a seminar in Canberra for the Risk Management Institution of Australasia (RMIA) called 'How to Be Heard'. At the time I was the President of their NSW chapter and the most common question I was asked by members was, 'How do I get the CEO to listen to me?' The risk profession was shooting itself in the foot. For years we had many, many well-meaning people guiding the profession down a highly technical path. An international standard had just been released and risk terminology was flowing freely. Risk professionals inside organisations and consultants

7: Construct of a conversation

alike were creating more and more complex methodologies, because each iteration was considered an improvement.

And no one was listening.

It got to the point where if I met a CEO at an after-hours seminar and introduced myself as a risk consultant they would practically turn around and flee.

Part of the 'How to Be Heard' seminar was called 'From Risk-Speak to C-Suite Speak'. It was one of the most significant points on my journey to the development of my Winning Conversations Program. I'll never forget the lights going on for some very experienced risk professionals in the room. 'No wonder they aren't listening!'

Figure 7.1 shows two diagrams, the first representing the essence of the concept, the other giving an example. See, it isn't hard.

Figure 7.1: From risk-speak to C-suite speak

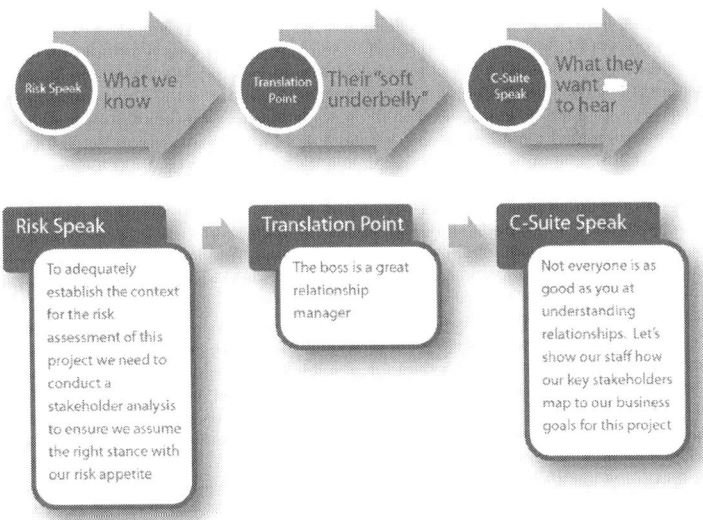

No matter what business you are in, no matter what your role, you will use jargon. If you are in a technical role, some people (you included) may be overcomplicating the process or message. Take some time to reflect on this now.

The rule of three

Picture yourself in a car yard. You are approached by a friendly salesperson. They ask what kind of car you are interested in. You tell them. They escort you to the latest model, let you have a look. You like what you see. They suggest you climb into the driver's seat. You do. You like the feel, the look, the idea of owning this car.

The salesperson, who can tell you are interested, starts listing all the benefits of the car. Having summed you up (rightly or wrongly), he says: 'You know, this is the most environmentally friendly six-cylinder car on the market, yet it can do zero to sixty in six seconds. And the boot [or trunk, if you are from North America] space is second to none.'

You are just about sold. Then the salesperson moves on. 'Not only that, but look at the interior. Leather seats, with seat warmers. And check out this sound system [blast of music!] Not to mention the...'

And your brain automatically brings up your protective shields. You start thinking, *if this car is so good, why does he have to keep listing its benefits?*

The rule of three has been broken. People like things in threes. Think of *The Three Little Pigs* or *The Three Musketeers*

7: Construct of a conversation

or Superman's 'truth, justice and the American way'. Or ask Shakespeare's Julius Caesar: 'Friends, Romans, Countrymen'; or advertisers: 'Slip, Slop, Slap' (a very successful government-funded campaign in Australia in the 1980s to shift people's attitudes to taking precautions against skin cancer).

We like things in threes. We just do. So when three benefits of the car were listed your interest was piqued. For every additional benefit claimed you felt increasingly sold to.

So stick to three.

And, by the way — any sales program will tell you this — don't sell features, sell value. For example, the car salesperson would have been better saying:

1. 'You know, the environment is so important to people these days and this car is the most environmentally friendly six-cylinder car on the market.'
2. 'Yet it still has plenty of acceleration when you need it for safety. You have to drive defensively, right?'
3. 'And the boot [trunk] is second to none. You can fit four school bags, four mini scooters and a beach bag in there, no problem. I know that from experience!'

Delivering bad news

Giving bad news in a conversation is one of the toughest things to do. I don't consider firing someone a 'conversation', so I don't mean that kind of bad news. I mean the kind that relates to the decision your audience needs to make. For example, your advice may be to withdraw from the market a product that was only recently launched, or to change the advice given to the minister's office, or to cease running a fundraising event that was one of the foundations of the charity because it is outdated and no longer brings sufficient rewards.

In these types of situations you *must* start with positives. Follow the steps shown in Figure 7.2. Take the product withdrawal, for example. You might focus on what had been learned from the process and how the role the person played in the product launch made that learning possible.

Figure 7.2: Delivering bad news

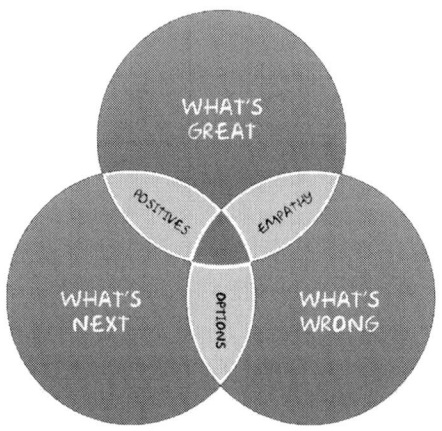

Then deliver the bad news with empathy. 'Despite what we all agreed was a great idea, despite the research and prototyping, and your considerable leadership on this one, I can't see how we can continue. I think it's time to change direction.'

Then provide options for moving forward so they are part of the decision, if not the decision maker. The options could focus on how other benefits can be pursued through the announcement of the withdrawal, or on which new products can now be fast-tracked using the resources that have been freed up.

This is a situation in which using some of the creative thinking techniques from the section on developing adaptability in chapter 6 could come in nicely.

Painting your picture

But I can't draw! I used to tell myself this. Now I draw all the time. As I mentioned earlier, all the hand drawings in this book are by me. I wish they were tidier and more artistic, but they're not. Still, I have found drawing diagrams a potent tool. Let me remind you why.

When I draw diagrams for people in a one-on-few meeting I draw them on an A4 sheet to give me plenty of room. I also use a four-colour pen. This lets me highlight common themes or differences between things that otherwise seem quite similar.

Also look to 'script' how you describe your model. If you're really serious you might write and memorise your script. Over time your delivery will become more natural. Most effective is if you describe your model while you are drawing it.

If you don't have paper, use your tablet. Worse comes to worst, draw on the back of a napkin. Literally. More on that in the resources section at the end of this chapter.

Telling your story

When you tell a story in a conversation there are three rules to remember:

Rule 1: Not too long and detailed. Let them fill in the gaps in their head. They will get further into the story if some non-key elements are left to their imagination.

Rule 2: Be prepared with two-minute, one-minute and 30-second versions. If your meeting has been shortened, you won't want to miss the opportunity of giving your advice, as you may not get another opportunity. If your story and picture are good enough, the meeting will be extended or a second meeting scheduled.

Rule 3: Look them in the eye. The emotion you feel in telling your story will be communicated to them through eye contact. In turn, emotion will show in their eyes that you will instinctively feed off. Emotional engagement will increase in both of you.

Making them believe

While bringing your wisdom to the table for your winning conversation, you also need to be prepared for when your audience does not buy in straight away. Remember, people will sometimes raise protective barriers against your advice, and the Pathfinder Model is about helping you navigate around them. Some put up more barriers than others, though. Some, for example, won't revise their position or their beliefs without a fight. **So you need to be ready for the counterpunch.**

If you have truly stood in their shoes, you should be able to anticipate the counter-arguments they might make. Write them down in advance and work on your replies. You may need statistics, case studies, another diagram to draw to show the weakness in their argument, or another story, metaphor or analogy that will cast it in a different light.

One last thing. Unless it is absolutely necessary, don't leave the meeting with more work to do; that is, don't let them use the need for more information as an excuse for not making a decision. If you have done your job, all the important evidence will be there. Ask them what they believe is missing and if it amounts to little of significance, suggest that further research would not be time well spent. If you can, turn the need for more information into an investigation of the best of the options you have put forward.

'Conversing' with a larger group

Here are some tips to create the same 'look and feel' of a conversation when you are interacting with a larger group:

1. Facilitate. When doing so your aim should be to stimulate the conversation. Protect people from being overridden by the boss or the most opinionated participant. Draw out their thoughts, positive and negative, on your advice. It's good to know what is working and what you still need to deal with.
2. Use a whiteboard, rather than a PowerPoint presentation. While not as effective as writing on the back of a napkin, it has a more intimate and inclusive effect than PowerPoint.

3. If you have to use PowerPoint, use its design and animation features. The new design features in PowerPoint allow you to create much more engaging presentations. With the animation features you can step through a diagram, building it step by step, just as though you were drawing it on a whiteboard.

Plunging in

It's time for you to take the plunge. The more often you have used the Pathfinder Model, the more Stand, Paint, Tell and Make tools and techniques you have mastered, the more plunging in will feel just like taking a dip in the pool on a hot day. To help build your confidence, the final chapter provides concrete examples of the Pathfinder Model in action.

Chapter summary

In this chapter I have given you a series of tips to help you deliver in those vitally important 15 minutes of a winning conversation. These include using the Pathfinder tools, being aware of the importance of first impressions, listening carefully, using language appropriate to your audience and learning how to deliver bad news. Use this chapter as a checklist every time you prepare for a challenging conversation, until these techniques become second nature.

Recommended resources

Oscar Trimboli. Deep Listening Podcast. www.oscartrimboli.com

Ernesto Sirolli (2012). 'Want to help someone? Shut up and Listen!' TED Talk.

Bryan Whitefield. 'How to Be Heard' webinar. www.bryanwhitefield.com

Carmine Gallo (2017) . 'In His Surprise TED Talk, Pope Francis Relied on This Proven Writing and Speaking Formula'. Inc.

8

The Pathfinder Model in practice

Practise before you preach

To help you on your journey to becoming persuasive, this chapter offers you some examples of the Pathfinder Model in action. I recommend you learn from them, work on your own suite of tools, and store them in one place so you can quickly pick and choose from them when preparing an approach to a new influencing situation. Then practise. The more naturally your delivery flows, the more effective your message will be. Afterwards, always conduct a post-mortem on how your approach worked and why. With lots of practice you will hone and develop your skills and become a more masterful influencer.

I have found that over time I have developed an almost intuitive skill in using the Pathfinder Model on the run in meetings. I have used S-curves and Venn diagrams so many times I can draw up something new on the spot. I have a suite of stories that I can adapt to any situation. Through the books, papers and case studies I have read, and my own direct experience, I have a cache of important statistics, facts and reference points embedded in my memory, ready for fast retrieval. Before entering into the Paint, Tell and Make stages of the Pathfinder Model, standing in my audience's shoes has become a very natural and automatic starting point for me.

Before we move on to the suite of practical examples, let me provide an example that was not inspired by the Pathfinder Model yet offers compelling evidence that using the tools and techniques outlined in this book can be very, very effective. It is the story of perhaps the most masterful influencers of all time, Indigenous Australian elders.

The Dreaming

Storytelling and artistic representation have sustained Australian Aboriginal culture for tens of thousands of years. Without books, film or advanced technology, the elders of each generation were able to pass on the most important cultural information not just to ensure survival, but also to sustain a social order that permitted their people to live in relative peace and harmony.

Helen McKay, of Australian Storytelling, writes, 'Dreamtime stories are the oral form of the spiritual Dreaming which comprises: Art: the visual form, Customs: the practical form, Dance: the physical form, Music: the acoustic form, Totems: the spiritual forms, Lore: the cultural form, Lands: the geographical forms. Altogether they form an all-encompassing, mystical whole: The Dreaming.'[26]

Let's look at the Dreaming through the prism of the Pathfinder Model.

The Dreaming and Aboriginal heritage

In Aboriginal tradition, elders who were entrusted with passing on tribal lore and customs to younger generations had a very serious responsibility. They needed to persuade children to embrace certain rules and behaviours and learn what would be expected of them as they grew older. To prepare them. They also needed to persuade young men and women to respect and maintain ancestral customs and to learn and remember important traditional practices, such as where and when to hunt, fish and gather food. Remember, despite their ancient traditions, over time much could change in their environment, for example as a result of cycles of drought or flood, and such cycles could take years or even decades to play out.

Stand in their shoes

Okay, you're right, they didn't actually wear shoes. You got me. But let's consider the idea metaphorically.

It was easy for Aboriginal elders to stand in the shoes of those they needed to persuade. They had been there. They well understood the drivers, from the need to survive to the search for friendship and love and every human impulse and emotion in between. More importantly, they knew what was at stake. They knew they had to align the needs and

8: The Pathfinder Model in practice

wants of the younger generations to their overall objective, which was the survival and security of the clan.

Paint them a picture

Aboriginal rock art is very well known. It is not hard to imagine an elder, with members of the tribe gathered around him or her to hear a Dreamtime story, using a stick to draw pictures in the sand. Picture how an elder might draw a topographical map of distant country where the tribe might need to venture someday if the drought didn't break or if the rains and flooding came again.

Tell them a story

Yes, of course they told stories, but let's have a look at how they were used. Take the story of the platypus.[27] In the version found at Didjshop, the main characters are a water rat named Bilargun and a duck named Daroo. The two married and had babies that had Daroo's webbed feet and Bilargun's fur coat and a flat tail. In the story Bilargun tells Daroo to hit her tail on the water to let him know if she is in danger. The story finishes with the key point that a platypus now hits its tail on the water to warn of danger.

So the platypus story has characters that bring the story to life. It has a key incident, which is the mating of Bilargun and Daroo to create the platypus. And it has a point: it teaches young hunters that the flapping of the platypus's tail means it has sensed danger.

Make them believe

The storyteller in Aboriginal culture had credibility and status. They held a position of authority in the tribe, so they had all the social proof they needed. Their credibility was validated because their stories were tried and proven as they were passed down from generation to generation.

If you are a CEO or equivalent

If you are a CEO or equivalent, I need to warn you that the following practical examples are directed to internal advisers in organisations, for two reasons — first, because they are the people I help most often, and secondly, because they are the people with the toughest job.

This may not be true for you, but many people in your shoes think the back office restricts business too much. They are the tree huggers from HR, the bean counters from finance, the colour-iners from the marketing department. **They are the creators of red tape!** The business, so this thinking goes, gets on with the business *despite* the back office. But you know the back office needs to shine, though. You know it needs to get things right, to help the business make good decisions. You know it needs to design blue ribbon processes and systems AND ensure they are perceived that way.

I hope the examples that follow are helpful not only for those from support functions, but also for the business the support functions serve.

Three practical persuasion examples

1. Risk management

Selling risk is the hardest job for any back-office person, because risk people are selling an intangible benefit. That is, if you listen to what I have to say you will make better decisions and will be better off. When things come out as planned we like to take personal credit. So how can we compare the world with and without a sound approach to risk management? Run two parallel universes, one with and one without risk management? The approach I have taken is to make the benefits of risk management tangible. Here's how.

The risk management journey

The risk journey for an organisation is from a place where risk is seen as a compliance function to a place where it is used to drive growth through well-considered risk taking. Here is how I explain it to senior leaders to get their buy-in.

Stand in their shoes

To demonstrate to a senior leadership group that I understand their challenges I use a story about David Thodey when he was CEO of Telstra. I was at a seminar where Thodey was being interviewed on stage. Asked about his biggest challenge in running such a large organisation, he replied along these lines: 'Ensuring that information that I need to know about gets through to me, past all the information people are trying give me that I don't need to know about, in time for me to do something about it.' I then explain how Thodey re-engineered the risk management function at Telstra and bolstered its ranks to help ensure the right information got to him in time.

Paint them a picture

To show my audience the journey I want to take them on I draw the following S-curve. I explain that rising up the middle of the curve is quick, once staff get the value and know what is required. Towards the top of the curve, though, it gets harder to get the full benefits. I go on to explain why.

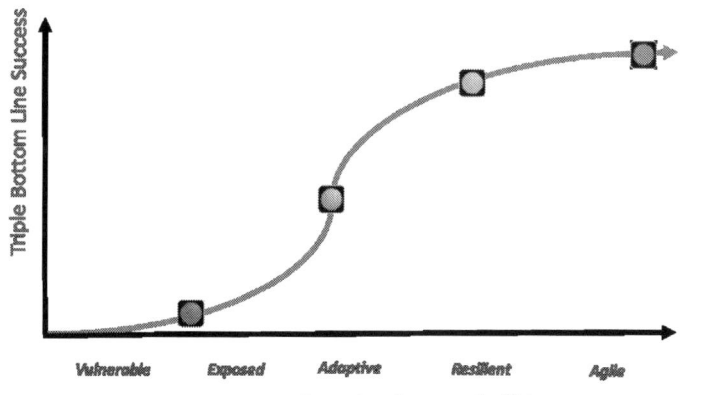

Tell them a story

I like to make a point about how we are good at managing the risks that hurt us last week and last month, and the ones that hurt us a lot last year, and that older organisations are good at managing risks that are burned into the corporate memory. I use the story of Disney Inc. They are very, very protective when it comes to accusations of copyright infringement. The reason for this is that the founder, Walt Disney, was sued early in the company's history, and the experience stuck with Walt for ever. And that was passed down through the generations of leaders that followed.

I then make the point that organisations are often not that great at identifying new risks before it is too late to manage them.

Make them believe

These days I have plenty of credibility in the risk space. I have written and video testimonials and have also written a book on managing risk in decision making. Nonetheless, I always do enough research on a client to make sure I can talk knowledgeably about them and their industry. This ensures my credibility remains strong.

2. Finance – budgeting

A common issue I have encountered with corporate service teams is a clear need to encourage the business to engage sooner with corporate services. Too often the internal service provider is expected to 'get it done' no matter how late in the day, because the 'business' is more important. With this kind of issue, finance is better placed than most, as everyone needs their budget signed off. Yet still managers will engage in the process only at the last minute. Here is an example of how you can approach your internal client to ensure early engagement.

Budgeting

Budgets have become increasingly rigid in organisations as stakeholders have called for more and more accurate forecasting so budgets can be reliably measured. Therefore managers have a vested interest in ensuring their budgets are approved.

Stand in their shoes

There's no big secret here. The one thing you need to understand about a particular manager is the extent to which their budgets are:

1. under pressure to be reduced, maintained or increased
2. highly variable and hence difficult to set.

From there you need to show empathy and a willingness to help.

Paint them a picture

The following diagram depicts the three phases of budget preparation — Formulation, Clarification and Negotiation — and the best trajectory to achieve a good outcome. It then shows the typical trajectory, beginning with a long period of inactivity, then a manic rush and a frustrating period of clarification and negotiation.

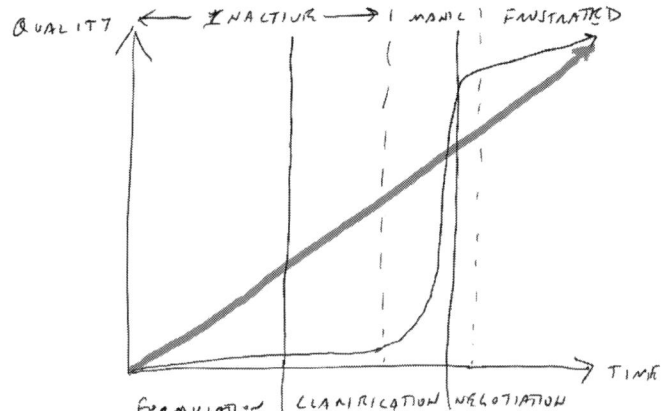

Tell them a story

I sometimes tell a story about a near-fatal car accident I had in northern Ontario in Canada, when I rolled a car into a snow bank and was left hanging upside down by my seatbelt. I had to dig snow *into* the car to edge my way out. Eventually I was picked up by a passing truck driver. The point I make is that I was speeding in unfamiliar conditions because I had unwisely left things to the last minute.

Make them believe

There are usually two opportunities here. One is to show you do truly understand the difficulty of their situation and the other is to demonstrate you have insights that can help them. For example, if you come with some analysis of their budgets showing how variable or not they have been and where they benchmark well or not so well against similar business functions, you will gain a level of respect and authority that will ensure your advice is well heeded.

3. Project portfolio management

Many organisations take a portfolio management approach to projects. Often housed within a corporate services or shared services function will be a Project Management Office (PMO). Their challenge is to ensure a good-quality and consistent approach to project management across the enterprise. Here is what one of my clients, Lloyd Dobson, came up with during the training program I ran for their corporate services team.

Project Management Maturity

Lloyd and his team were about to introduce a new approach to the management of projects across the enterprise. He wanted to get buy-in from the top ASAP.

Stand in their shoes

Lloyd had had enough conversations with the executive team to know their key focus was getting a better return on their investments in projects.

Paint them a picture

Lloyd and his team drew up the model below. They used a ladder model to show where the organisation was, that the goal was improved return on investment, and the various stages the project would take the organisation through to achieve this goal.

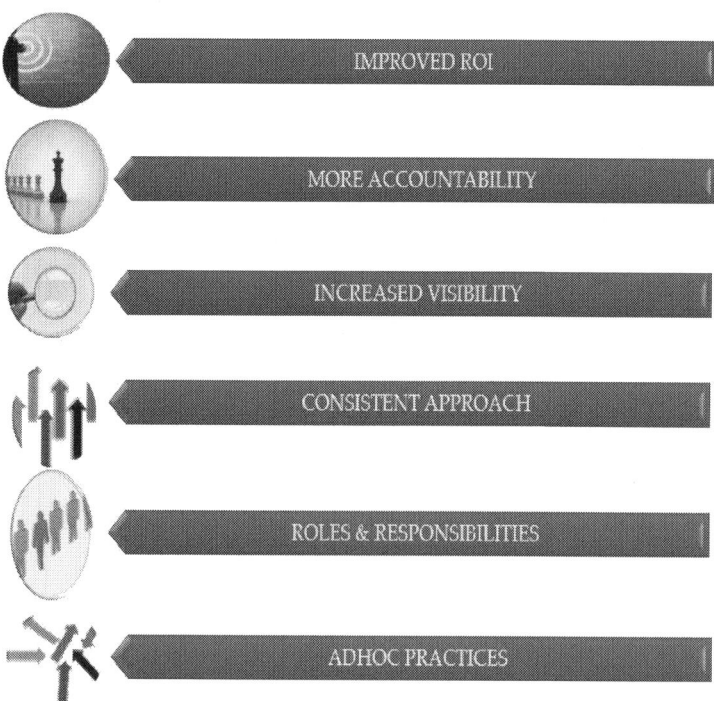

Tell them a story

Lloyd used a story about what it was like to be a football coach of young kids. Of how they start by kicking the ball in every direction, including into their own goal. He explained how he was able to get them moving the ball forward by giving them direction and roles and responsibilities. He linked his story to the current project management practices for demonstrating the benefits obtainable with a sound framework and a little coaching.

Make them believe

The make them believe part was still to come. However, his plan was to provide accurate and credible reporting to the Executive to provide a baseline to work from, and to show the scale of improvement over time when projects run well.

Recommended resources

Books

Allison, G. T., & Zelikow, P. (1999). *Essence of decision: Explaining the Cuban Missile Crisis*. New York, NY: Longman.

Carnegie, D. (1936). *How to Win Friends and Influence People*. New York, NY: Simon and Schuster.

Cialdini, R. B. (2006). *Influence: The Psychology of Persuasion*, revised edition. New York, NY: Harper Business.

Dowling, S. (2016). *Work with Me: How to get people to buy into your ideas*. Milton, QLD: John Wiley & Sons.

Heath, C., & Heath, D. (2013). *Decisive: How to make better choices in life and work*. New York: Crown Business.

Kahneman, D. (2011). *Thinking, Fast and Slow.* United States: Farrar, Straus and Giroux.

Maister, D. H., Green, C. H., & Galford, R. (2000). *The Trusted Advisor.* New York, NY: Free Press.

Nutt, P. (2002). *Why Decisions Fail: Avoiding the Blunders and Traps That Lead to Debacles.* United States: Berrett-Koehler.

Simon, H. A. (1947). *Administrative Behavior: A Study of Decision-Making Processes in Administrative Organization.* United States: Macmillan.

Sinek, S. (2009). *Start with Why: How great leaders inspire everyone to take action.* New York, NY: Portfolio.

Sobel, A., & Panas, J. (2012). *Power Questions: Build relationships, win new business, and influence others.* Hoboken, NJ: John Wiley & Sons.

Thaler, R. H., & Sunstein, C. R. (2009). Nud*ge: Improving decisions about health, wealth, and happiness.* New York, NY: Penguin.

Videos

Robert Cialdini on 'The Powers of Persuasion'.

'The Tiger That Came in for a Pint'. This is a wonderful piece of television that demonstrates what can be achieved in a graphic storybook. A combination of Paint and Tell.

Bryan Whitefield, 'How to Be Heard' (webinar): bryanwhitefield.com.

Bryan Whitefield, 'Becoming a Trusted Adviser: Gaining a Seat at the Table' (webinar): bryanwhitefield.com.

The wrap

A very important event on my journey to becoming a more persuasive adviser was meeting communication guru Matt Church, whom I mentioned in chapter 4, 'Painting pictures'. After participating in one of Matt's training programs I signed up for some one-on-one coaching. I showed him the tools I was then using to engage with senior leaders. One used an S-curve to depict the journey an organisation undertakes when implementing a risk management program. It starts slow and builds quickly in the middle, then it takes a heap of effort to gain the critical final benefits that mean it is embedded in everyday practice. I also told him the story I use to go along with the diagram.

Matt asked me if I had developed the diagram and story since attending his program. My answer was 'no'. He was suitably impressed. Through Matt's program and his coaching, I was beginning to understand why what I had been doing had been working so well. Even better, Matt suggested ways I could improve what was already succeeding for me. I still shake my head at the acceleration in my consulting practice that I experienced as a result.

The Pathfinder Model, designed to help you navigate past all the barriers people put up to protect themselves from bad advice, is the result of my unpacking what worked for me and reconstructing it as a simple process that anyone can follow. When combined with my MCI Decision Model, it allows you to go deep inside the heads of those you need to influence so you can have more winning conversations. Conversations in which you persuade others of your authority, so they follow your advice, learn to trust it and to trust you. As a trusted adviser, you will have earned a seat at the table, and people will seek out your advice. Then you will be able to make the impact you were born to make.

I wish you and those you lead alongside the very best in decision making. Because better decisions will inevitably lead to a better world for all of us.

If you enjoyed this book, you will also enjoy my blogs. I would love you to sign up at my website, www.bryanwhitefield.com.

Endnotes

1. Television and Radio Interview: *'After Two Years — a Conversation with the President'*, 17 December 1962. www.jfklibrary.org
2. Verling, John. November 2015. *Obama and Cuba Quotes: 10 Times President Has Spoken on Relations.* www.newsmax.com
3. Andrews, Travis M. *Emma Watson wins first major gender-neutral movie award for Beauty and the Beast.* May 2017. www.smh.com.au
4. Ibid.
5. Jared A. Nielsen, Brandon A. Zielinski, Michael A. Ferguson, Janet E. Lainhart, Jeffrey S. Anderson. *An Evaluation of the Left-Brain vs. Right-Brain Hypothesis with Resting State Functional Connectivity Magnetic Resonance Imaging.* PLOS One, August 2013.
6. Farnworth, Demian. *Empathy Maps: A Complete Guide to Crawling Inside Your Customer's Head.* August 2014. www.Copyblogger.com
7. Gray, Dave. *Updated Empathy Map Canvas.* July 2017. www.medium.com
8. Iannarino, Anthony. *Win More by Serving Your Buyers Where They Are.* April 2016. www.thesalesbog.com
9. Many of us know a basic history of DISC, but did you know that the basic theory behind the four quadrants of DISC Personality Styles actually can be traced all the way back to 444 B.C.? www.discinsights.com
10. *MBTI Basics.* www.myersbriggs.org
11. Ibid.
12. *What is DISC Overview.* www.discprofiles.com
13. *Understanding DISC Profiles.* www.discprofiles.com
14. Belot, Henry. *ATO urges staff to dob in colleagues who take long lunches, read paper at work.* February 2018. www.abc.net.au
15. *Active Learning.* www.changingminds.org
16. Jeffrey D. Wammes, Melissa E. Meade & Myra A. Fernandes, *The drawing effect: Evidence for reliable and robust memory benefits in free recall.* University of Waterloo. April 2016. www.youtube.com
17. *Draw a Graduation Cap.* www.wiki.how.com

18 *4mat a natural learning cycle.* www.4mat.eu
19 www.enchantedlearning.com
20 *Why people believe they can't draw - and how to prove they can.* Graham Shaw. TEDxHull. April 2015.
21 Dolan, G. (2017). *Stories for Work: The essential guide to business storytelling.* Wiley.
22 Carnegie, D. (1936). How to Win Friends and Influence People. New York, N.Y.: Simon and Schuster.
23 *John Lithgow talks "Stories by Heart" on Broadway.* www.cbsnews.com
24 Werner, Joel. *1.0 Shoal Attack!* September 2017. www.abc.net.au
25 Malcolm, Lynne. *First impressions — the face bias.* July 2017. www.abc.net.au
26 McKay, Helen. *Australian Aboriginal Storytelling.* www.australianstorytelling.org.au
27 *Bilargun and Daroo 'The Platypus story'.* www.didjshop.com

Made in the USA
San Bernardino, CA
06 August 2019